GARY L. GASTINEAU, DONALD J. SMITH,
AND REBECCA TODD, CFA

RISK MANAGEMENT, DERIVATIVES, AND FINANCIAL ANALYSIS UNDER SFAS NO. 133

THE RESEARCH FOUNDATION OF AIMR
AND BLACKWELL SERIES IN FINANCE

Gary L. Gastineau
Nuveen Investments

Donald J. Smith
Boston University

Rebecca Todd, CFA
Boston University

Risk Management, Derivatives, and Financial Analysis under SFAS No. 133

**The Research Foundation of AIMR™
and Blackwell Series in Finance**

Research Foundation Publications

Risk Management, Derivatives, and Financial Analysis under SFAS No. 133

To obtain the *AIMR Publications Catalog,* contact:
AIMR, P.O. Box 3668, Charlottesville, Virginia 22903, U.S.A.
Phone 804-951-5499; Fax 804-951-5262; E-mail info@aimr.org
or
visit AIMR's World Wide Web site at www.aimr.org
to view the AIMR publications list.

ISBN 0-943205-51-4

Printed in the United States of America

February 2001

3 2280 00759 9228

Editorial Staff
Maryann Dupes
Editor

Lisa S. Medders
Assistant Editor

Jaynee M. Dudley
Production Manager

Kelly T. Bruton/Lois A. Carrier
Composition

Mission

The Research Foundation's mission is to identify, fund, and publish research that is relevant to the AIMR Global Body of Knowledge and useful for AIMR member investment practitioners and investors.

Biographies

Gary L. Gastineau is managing director of Exchange-Traded Funds at Nuveen Investments and a member of the Editorial Board of the *Financial Analysts Journal*. He received his A.B. in economics from Harvard College and his M.B.A. from Harvard Business School.

Donald J. Smith is an associate professor of finance and economics at the School of Management, Boston University, and a member of the Board of Advisors to the International Association of Financial Engineers. He received his M.B.A. and Ph.D. in economic analysis and policy from the School of Business Administration, University of California at Berkeley.

Rebecca Todd, CFA, is an associate professor in the Accounting Department of the Boston University School of Management and a member of the Financial Accounting Policy Committee of the Association for Investment Management and Research. She received her bachelor's degree in physics and master's degree in accounting from Old Dominion University and her Ph.D. in business administration from the Kenan-Flagler School of Business, University of North Carolina at Chapel Hill.

Contents

Foreword

Managing financial risk by using derivatives is a well-established practice of corporate management. During the past decade, however, risk management with derivatives has become increasingly sophisticated, which has greatly increased the complexity of financial analysis. Moreover, prior to Statement of Financial Accounting Standards (SFAS) No. 133, *Accounting for Derivative Instruments and Hedging Activities*, financial analysts were challenged not only by the increasing complexity of derivative transactions but also by inadequate disclosure of derivative exposures and transactions in financial statements. The well-publicized derivative debacles in the mid-1990s provided the impetus for the Financial Accounting Standards Board (FASB) to expedite its consideration of derivative accounting and to introduce SFAS No. 133.

Gary L. Gastineau, Donald J. Smith, and Rebecca Todd's excellent monograph provides a remarkably accessible guide to the intricacies of SFAS No. 133. Moreover, it offers a clear and well-organized overview of the essential elements of risk management. The authors succinctly describe the nuances of arbitrage, hedging, insurance, and speculation, and they distinguish internal from external hedging. In addition to addressing some of the technical details of risk management, the authors tackle the philosophical challenge of Modigliani and Miller (M&M). In the idealized world of M&M, firms have no need to engage in risk management because investors can leverage or deleverage their exposure to firms more efficiently by managing risk at the portfolio level. Gastineau, Smith, and Todd take the reader beyond the abstract world of M&M and discuss how risk management is used to reduce taxable income, to lessen the probability of financial distress, and to stabilize cash flows in order to enable uninterrupted profitable investment.

Gastineau, Smith, and Todd decipher SFAS No. 133 against the backdrop of previous FASB standards (SFAS No. 52 and SFAS No. 80) so that the reader better understands the motivation of the FASB and the contributions of SFAS No. 133. They offer easy-to-follow examples of the various types of hedges addressed by SFAS No. 133 (fair value, cash flow, and currency), and they describe in detail the characteristics that qualify a financial instrument as a derivative instrument and the conditions that require bifurcation of embedded options. They discuss these issues not in an abstract way but within the context of several well-publicized debacles, including Gibson Greetings, Orange County, and Procter & Gamble. Where applicable, they point out how SFAS No. 133 might have prevented these unfortunate experiences. They also introduce a hypothetical company to illustrate certain principles that are not relevant to these actual examples.

Finally, Gastineau, Smith, and Todd do not shy away from critiquing SFAS No. 133. In addition to their thoroughness in highlighting its benefits, they are quick to warn analysts of its limitations. This monograph is indispensable to anyone who relies on financial statements or engages in risk management with derivatives. The Research Foundation is pleased to present *Risk Management, Derivatives, and Financial Analysis under SFAS No. 133.*

Mark P. Kritzman, CFA
Research Director
The Research Foundation of the
Association for Investment Management and Research

Acknowledgments

The authors gratefully acknowledge important comments and contributions from Ira Kawaller of Kawaller & Company, Michael Joseph of Ernst & Young, and an anonymous referee. The authors, of course, remain responsible for any errors or omissions.

1. Introduction

Risk management is all about the trade-offs between financial risk and reward that inevitably face a firm's managers, its board of directors, and ultimately its shareholders. Although risk management is a latecomer to the *theory* of corporate finance, it is not new to the *practice* of corporate finance. Long before the word "derivative" was ever used in financial circles, managers were weighing returns and risks when making decisions affecting the firm, such as whether to expand, how to invest the firm's capital, and whether to issue debt or equity.

Nearly all management decisions, including risk management decisions, affect a firm's financial health, and the window to the outside world of a firm's financial health is its financial statements. Since the days of Graham and Dodd, financial analysts have pushed for transparency of financial statements. Unfortunately, the use of risk management practices in general (and derivatives in particular) has gone largely unreported in financial statements—to the dismay of financial analysts and contrary to their ideal of transparency.

To further complicate the situation, the available evidence from surveys of market practice indicates that firms use a rather *ad hoc* approach to risk management. Although some firms manage foreign exchange, interest rate, and commodity price risk carefully with an eye on cash flows and the timing of investment outlays, many are selecting their hedge ratios based at least in part on their views of future market conditions. Many firms evaluate the risk management function with an eye on how the derivative contracts themselves perform—not necessarily on the combined result of the derivatives and the underlying exposures. Although this practice might be called "strategic hedging" by the firm, it also indicates a speculative side to derivative use that is of concern to financial analysts.

The Financial Accounting Standards Board (FASB) has issued Statement of Financial Accounting Standards (SFAS) No. 133, *Accounting for Derivative Instruments and Hedging Activities*, to add transparency to a firm's use of derivatives and its risk management practices.[1] As is often the case, variability still remains in how firms apply these standards to their financial statements, and the end result thus falls short of the goal.

---

[1]FASB statements may be obtained from its Web site (www.fasb.org) or by contacting the FASB in Norwalk, CT.

In this monograph, we attempt to explain for the financial analyst a firm's use of risk management practices and how those practices can be accounted for under SFAS No. 133. We cover the practical and theoretical basis for risk management in Chapter 2 and report on the results of several surveys and other evidence of corporate risk management practices. In Chapter 3, we delve into how a firm's use of derivatives affects financial analysis and why the FASB consequently saw a need to reform accounting for derivatives. Chapter 4 covers the intricacies of SFAS No. 133, and Chapter 5 provides examples of financial statement analysis for firms complying with SFAS No. 133. Finally, Chapter 6 summarizes the objectives of SFAS No. 133 and its significance for financial analysts.

Although this monograph is not an exhaustive analysis of risk management, derivatives, or SFAS No. 133's impact on financial statements (and hence financial analysts), we hope that the reader will come away more informed and better able to evaluate a firm's risk management practices and financial statements that record the use of derivatives.

2. Corporate Risk Management: Practice and Theory

Risk management is the process of assessing and modifying—on an ongoing basis—the many trade-offs between risk and reward that face a firm. These trade-offs can be evaluated based on whether they are done for the purpose of hedging, speculation, or arbitrage. Equally important are the practical and theoretical objectives of a corporate risk management program.

Risk–Return Trade-Offs

One of the first lessons that a student of finance learns is that higher expected returns are accompanied by higher levels of risk. The corollary is that risk reduction typically entails some cost in the form of lower expected returns.

Panel A in **Figure 2.1** illustrates the classic risk–reward trade-off and introduces three key terms: "hedging," "speculation," and "arbitrage." The initial position reflects the current status of the firm. Reward is some measure of an outcome whereby more is better than less; an economist might call the measure of reward "utility," and a chief financial officer might call it "earnings per share." Risk registers the degree of certainty about attaining the expected level of reward. More risk, moving to the right in the figure, spreads out the probability distribution for given outcomes. Moving to the left tightens the distribution, indicating greater certainty. This spreading out and tightening of the probability distribution is illustrated in Panel B as a range of outcomes plus and minus one standard deviation from the expected level of the reward. The risk-free reward is the result when no uncertainty exists as to the outcome. Note that the initial position might be right where the firm wants to be in terms of its potential risk and reward. Thus, sometimes effective risk management entails not taking any further action.

Hedging. Actions taken to reduce risk are known broadly as hedging. Such actions include diversification, buying options or insurance contracts, and using forward and futures contracts to lock in a subsequent price or rate on a transaction. The common denominator is the intent to reduce risk and make the reward outcome more certain. Note that some people distinguish between hedging and insuring (see, for instance, Bodie and Merton's 2000 textbook, *Finance*). Hedging, in the sense that Bodie and Merton use it, is limited to securing a future price, thereby eliminating potential gain as well

Figure 2.1. The Risk–Reward Trade-Off

A. Hedging, Speculation, and Arbitrage

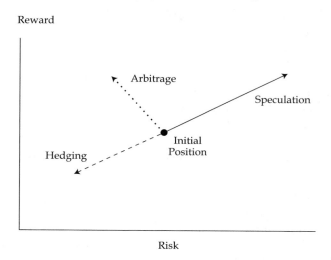

B. Effect of Increasing Risk on the Probability Distribution

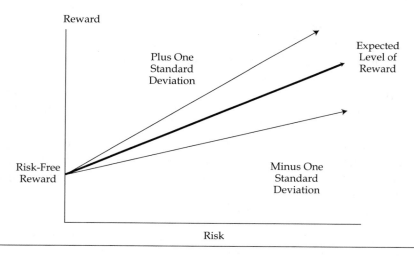

as loss. Insuring against a loss provides protection from adverse price movement while retaining potential benefit (i.e., if the option is not needed). The broader use of the term "hedging," which we adopt here, follows accounting terminology and applies to options as well as forwards, futures, and swaps.

A useful distinction to make is between *internal* and *external* hedging activities. Internal hedging involves asset and liability selection—for instance, managing credit risk by setting exposure limits with specific customers and managing foreign exchange (FX) risk by raising funds in currencies for which the enterprise has net operating revenues. Another example of internal hedging is interest rate immunization, whereby the risk characteristics (i.e., the duration statistics) of assets and liabilities are intentionally matched. The underlying risk could be operational, rather than strictly financial. For instance, a firm could choose to diversify across production technologies or energy sources. The key feature is that internal hedging happens naturally in the course of making routine investment and financing decisions and often appears without comment in financial statements.

In contrast, external hedging involves the acquisition of a derivative financial contract having a payoff that is negatively correlated with an existing exposure. These derivatives can be exchange traded or obtained in the over-the-counter (OTC) market. They can have symmetrical payoffs (like those of futures, forwards, and swaps) or asymmetrical payoffs (like those of options). The derivatives can be embedded in an asset or liability (e.g., a callable bond) or can be stand-alone instruments. In any case, the external hedge involves a transaction that is not itself part of ordinary business operations and decisions and often has not been accounted for directly on the balance sheet.

A payoff matrix is a handy way to summarize a risk management problem. Suppose that a firm's main risk exposure is to volatile corn prices; the firm buys corn on the open market and then makes and sells corn products. The firm has learned that it cannot easily pass higher input prices on to customers. The matrix for the ensuing production cycle is shown in **Exhibit 2.1**. Note that the risky event is an *unexpected change* in the level of future corn prices. A principle of risk management is that one cannot do anything about events that are already widely anticipated and priced into derivative products. Therefore, the risky event is not that corn input prices increase but that corn input prices turn out to be higher than expected (or, more technically, above the level priced into the forward curve for corn).

In this example, the essence of the external hedging problem is to have a gain on the derivative contract offset the loss when corn prices rise. The firm

---

Exhibit 2.1. Effect on Underlying Exposure and Hedge Contract from Risky Event

Risky Event	Underlying Exposure	Hedge Contract
Corn input prices unexpectedly rise	Loss	Gain
Corn input prices unexpectedly fall	Gain	Loss

could execute the hedge internally by buying corn in the spot market and storing it as inventory until needed. Instead, the firm executes an external hedge by going long (i.e., buying) some corn futures (or forward contracts).[1] Note that use of a futures contract in this example represents "synthetic inventory" in that it is a way for the firm to assure itself of the availability and the cost of an input (i.e., corn) to the production process.

An inevitable, yet fundamental, decision facing the firm is whether to use a futures or option contract to carry out the external hedge. In this example of corn price risk, a call option on spot market corn (or a call on corn futures) provides the needed gain to offset the loss if prices rise. The key difference between futures and options is how the firm feels about taking a loss on the derivative if corn prices fall. The call option limits that loss to the premium paid for the insurance, regardless of how low the corn price turns out to be. The loss on the futures, however, depends on the actual drop in the spot corn price. Thus, perhaps the best way to distinguish futures from options is how much and when one pays for the needed payoff. With an option, that amount is certain and is paid up front. With a forward contract, that amount is price contingent and time deferred because it is paid at the settlement (or delivery) date. With futures, the amount is path dependent and paid daily, depending on the extent of the day-to-day price movement.

This hedging problem of forwards versus options is illustrated in **Figure 2.2**. Notice that one factor in choosing between entering the long forward contract and buying the call option is the price that the hedger believes will prevail relative to the break-even price. If the hedger believes the price will be above breakeven, the forward is preferable. But if the hedger expects the price to be below breakeven, the option is the better choice. Even if vagueness about future prices is the motive for hedging, how one executes the hedge can be based on that vague view.

Speculation. Speculation is an action to increase expected reward, even though it raises the degree of uncertainty about achieving that outcome—a classic movement up and out in the reward–risk trade-off space. It is unlikely that a corporation would use the word "speculation" in describing its risk management strategy, and it is certainly possible that the risk-taking activity is not only reasonable but also appropriate. There is no reason to believe that the firm's initial position in Panel A of Figure 2.1 is optimal; that point on the trade-off line is simply where the corporation happens to be, not necessarily

---

[1]Futures are essentially exchange-traded forward contracts. Futures are standardized to facilitate trading on the exchange and are marked-to-market daily, with day-to-day gains and losses settled into a margin account to minimize credit risk.

Figure 2.2. Payoffs for Forward vs. Option Contracts

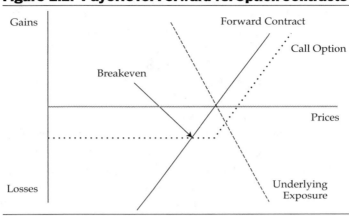

where its directors and management want it to be. An obvious example of an initial position is the point where an all-equity-financed firm starts to use leverage. Risk goes up from the use of debt financing, but the firm views the increase in expected reward to be worth the risk that the inability to service the debt will lead to bankruptcy. We discuss optimal capital structure and the role of risk management later in this chapter.

Risk management can be defined in an offhand manner as keeping (or increasing) the risks that are wanted and hedging away those that are not wanted. That choice ultimately goes to the perceived core competencies of the firm. Shareholders surely want the firm to bear certain business risks, which is why the investment is made in the first place, but shareholders do not want the firm to speculate in markets where it has no competitive advantage in terms of access to information or preferential transaction costs. But it is not hard to imagine a circumstance in which a firm commits the requisite human resources, technology, and financial capital in expectation of obtaining a profit on its speculative activities. An example of such a situation is a U.S. money-center bank that takes a position on an impending U.S. Federal Reserve action. The bank not only has professional "Fed watchers" on staff but also might believe that it has an early read on economic conditions through the many transactions of its corporate and retail customers.

A firm choosing to speculate should weigh the reward–risk trade-off carefully. That statement sounds obvious enough, but failure to weigh the consequences (arguably) lies at the heart of some of the infamous "derivative debacles" of the 1990s—for instance, Orange County, California's investment strategy. Orange County used extensive leverage to build up its holdings of structured notes containing embedded derivatives, in particular, inverse floating-rate notes. Such notes have coupon rate formulas, for instance 10 percent *minus* LIBOR (the London Interbank Offered Rate). When interest rates rose in 1994, the market value of these inverse floaters (as well as more traditional fixed-income securities) fell dramatically. Orange County ended up declaring bankruptcy with losses of about $1.7 billion on its investments. (See Jorion's 1995 book aptly titled *Big Bets Gone Bad* for a further description.)

The Orange County Investment Pool definitely was speculating in the hope of obtaining a higher rate of return for its depositors. One way to interpret the debacle is that the investment manager seriously misread the trade-off between reward and risk. **Figure 2.3** illustrates the misconception graphically. Management apparently thought it took on only a small amount of additional risk to get the higher expected returns (shown by the dotted line in the figure). But because of faulty or absent analysis of the possibility of higher interest rates and the fund's ability to "weather the storm" if rates rose, the investment risk in the strategy actually was much more unfavorable than management perceived (the dashed line shown in the figure).

Arbitrage. Arbitrage opportunities—circumstances in which a higher expected reward is not offset by higher risk—are the Holy Grail for financial managers. Note that this is not the textbook definition of arbitrage, which

Figure 2.3. Perceived and Actual Risk–Return for the Orange County Investment Pool

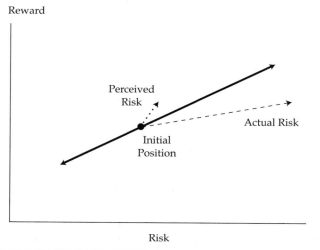

would entail a *riskless* exploitation of a violation of the law of one price.[2] In practice, arbitrage trades typically entail bearing some risk, for instance, the credit risk of a swap counterparty or the settlement risk on cross-border transactions. Thus, in this monograph, arbitrage simply implies a "northwest" movement from the initial position in Panel A of Figure 2.1.

A reasonably efficient financial marketplace should preclude persistent arbitrage opportunities. The very presence of an opportunity should set off market forces that would lead to the elimination of the arbitrage gain. Nevertheless, a much touted application of interest rate swaps over the years has been to lower a firm's cost of funds by issuing floating-rate debt and then converting it to a fixed rate (an apparent arbitrage opportunity). This swap is pictured in **Figure 2.4**. The firm raises funds at a floating rate of LIBOR plus 0.25 percent and enters a swap with a counterparty to pay a fixed rate of 7.00 percent and receive LIBOR. The all-in, synthetic fixed-rate cost of funds is 7.25 percent (neglecting any minor differences resulting from day-count conventions and assuming that the notional principal on the swap equals the par value on the debt). If the firm's direct fixed cost of funds is 7.40 percent, then a 15 basis point gain appears to be attributable to arbitrage.

Figure 2.4. Swapping Floating Rate for Fixed Rate

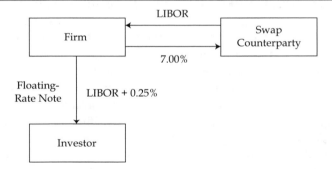

But before attributing those 15 basis points to arbitrage, one must remember that the swap entails bearing counterparty credit risk. To be specific, the firm's risk is that the counterparty defaults at a time when the swap would have to be replaced at a higher fixed rate than the firm is currently paying. That risk, which could be deemed to be statistically low, nevertheless has some value. The point is that the "arbitrage gain" is overestimated at 15 basis

---

[2]The law of one price states that the same item, or closely equivalent items, must sell for the same price, or related prices, in the marketplace at the same time.

points. The cost of default-risk insurance (a type of credit derivative), whether or not purchased, should be subtracted from that 15 basis points when measuring the benefit of the swap.

Objectives of Corporate Risk Management

Looking at the risk–reward trade-offs is an important step in evaluating a firm's risk management practices, but it is not the only step that should be taken. One must also look at the objectives of a risk management program. Unfortunately, as is often the case, practice and theory differ as to what those objectives are or should be.

The Practical Problem. The most basic, and perhaps the most difficult and most important, aspect of corporate risk management is the statement of objectives. That statement will guide the identification and measurement of risks and all the subsequent decisions in managing the risk–reward trade-offs, such as what percentage of the exposure to a specific risk to hedge and which derivatives to use. Risk managers cannot simply be told to reduce volatility, because the natural question is the volatility of what? Earnings per share? Share price? Net operating income? After-tax cash flow?

To illustrate the importance of the statement of objectives, consider a simple banking example. **Exhibit 2.2** displays the balance sheet for a simple bank. The only asset is a $100 million, 5-year, nonamortizing, commercial loan at 8 percent. The loan is funded by a $40 million, 1-year certificate of deposit (CD) at 6 percent and a $60 million, 10-year bond at 7 percent. The market value of each security is equal to its par value. Is this bank exposed to risk from higher or lower interest rates? If it were to hedge its risk, would it buy or sell interest rate futures contracts? The answer to both questions is that it depends on the objectives of the bank's management and directors.

At the danger of vast oversimplification, two different approaches exist for managing risk—one focusing on current market values and the other on net profit flows (either in cash or in accounting reports of profit and loss). The first seeks to smooth out movements in values that appear on the balance sheet. Its orientation is to the liquidation or current market value of the firm. The concern is that unexpected movements in FX and interest rates and/or

---

Exhibit 2.2. Balance Sheet for Simple Bank

Assets	Liabilities
$100 million, 5-year commercial loan at 8%	$40 million, 1-year CD at 6%
	$60 million, 10-year bond at 7%

---

commodity prices will reduce the current market value of the firm. Risk is measured with such metrics as value at risk (VAR) or in the case of interest rate risk, the gap between the duration of assets and liabilities.[3] A classic example of this approach is the manner in which a professional money manager assesses portfolio risk; what matters is the net asset value of the fund and how much it might drop if the market moves the wrong way.

The second, or net profit flow, approach seeks to smooth out volatility based on items that appear on the income statement using a measure such as earnings before interest and taxes or net operating cash flow. This approach considers the firm to be an ongoing operating institution. Risk is measured by the impact of unexpected rate and price movements on flow variables, such as net operating income and interest expense. Financial institutions have long used versions of this approach by identifying risk as arising from the mismatch in the amount of assets and liabilities maturing or from having their interest rates reset in given time periods.

Returning to the simple bank epitomized in Exhibit 2.2, one can clearly see that if the focus is on the income statement, the risk exposure is to higher interest rates. In particular, the exposure over the next five years is to higher CD rates that would reduce the bank's net interest margin. Assuming annual payments on the commercial loan and the bond, the profit turns into a loss if the one-year CD rate exceeds 9.5 percent. If a futures contract on one-year CDs happened to be traded, the bank could go short to hedge its borrowing rate risk.[4] The bank could lock in its sequential CD refunding rates in various ways by using either a strip hedge (having a sequence of future delivery or rollover dates) or a stack hedge (concentrating on a single delivery date). In sum, the bank would be *selling* interest rate futures to hedge the risk of having to pay higher interest rates.

Suppose that instead of focusing on continuing operations, the owner of the bank plans to divest fully, either by selling the bank outright or by selling the loan and using the proceeds to buy back the outstanding liabilities. In this circumstance, the interest rate risk exposure is toward lower, not higher, rates. This conclusion can be confirmed by simulation. Assume that all market

---

[3] Duration is a statistic commonly used in bond analysis to estimate the change in market value given a change in market yields. VAR analysis goes "beyond duration" to include the correlation of different asset returns in addition to their variances. VAR provides a summary number for potential loss subject to a specified degree of statistical confidence. We discuss VAR further in Chapter 6.

[4] Presumably, this contract would be like the eurodollar contract traded on the Chicago Mercantile Exchange. The futures price would be quoted at 100 minus the futures rate. Therefore, the seller of the contract would gain when rates rise and the futures price falls.

yields suddenly shift down by 100 basis points. The loan increases in market value to $104,100,197 (assuming annual payments and a new yield of 7 percent on comparable loans). The cost to buy back the CD would be $40,380,952 (the present value of $42.4 million, which is the future payoff on the CD given the 6 percent rate discounted at a new market rate of 5 percent). The cost to buy back the bond would be $64,416,052 (the market value of the bond at a new yield of 6 percent, assuming annual coupon payments). The net value of the bank falls by $696,807 ($104,100,197 − $40,380,952 − $64,416,052).

Duration analysis confirms this exposure to lower rates. The standard (or Macaulay) duration of the assets is 4.31, whereas the average duration of the liabilities is 4.91. This average is computed as the weighted average of the duration of the CD (which is 1.00) and the bond (which is 7.52) and using the shares of market value as the weights. Because the duration of assets is less than the average duration of liabilities, the bank would stand to gain value if interest rates were to rise. The market value of the loan would go down, but the cost to buy back the liabilities would fall even more. To hedge the risk of lower-than-expected interest rates, the bank would need to *buy* interest rate futures contracts. The bank would gain on those derivatives if rates fell and futures prices rose. This example illustrates that depending on what the bank perceives to be its risk management problem, it could conceivably either *buy* or *sell* futures contracts to solve that problem.

The Academic Perspective. The starting place for academic analysis of risk management is typically the seminal work of Modigliani and Miller (1958) on corporate finance and optimal capital structure. In particular, Modigliani and Miller (M&M) find that under a particular set of assumptions, the value of a firm does not depend on how the firm happens to be financed. In other words, the market value of the firm depends on the left side of the balance sheet and not on the composition of the right side. The financing decision between debt and equity becomes one of the famous M&M irrelevancy propositions.

A key part of the M&M analysis is the set of assumptions that drive the results. These strict assumptions include no taxation, no bankruptcy costs, and well-diversified investors. The central argument is that investors can create the same set of payoffs by leveraging their own portfolios as the firm can if it issues debt. Because investors can replicate, as well as undo, the financing decisions of the firm, leveraging the firm's balance sheet cannot itself be a source of value.

A corollary to the M&M conclusion is that risk management does not have any role in a firm that aims to maximize shareholder value. Investors will place no value on having management expend resources to reduce risks that can be hedged more efficiently by shareholders who simply hold a well-diversified portfolio of corporate shares. Shareholders already can hedge their financial risks by diversification, and any shareholders seeking to bear more risk can make the necessary asset allocation decisions themselves. It follows that, although the firm might still be interested in arbitrage applications for derivatives, no shareholder welfare motivation exists to reduce (or increase) the volatility of asset values or cash flows arising from the underlying core lines of business.

The academic perspective to corporate risk management typically accepts the M&M propositions as the baseline result but then proceeds to identify circumstances that justify hedging when the restrictive M&M assumptions are relaxed. The conclusion is that risk management can add value, in theory, if it reduces expected tax liabilities or bankruptcy costs or if investors do not hold diversified portfolios.[5]

Suppose that the tax schedule facing a firm is progressive, meaning that the marginal tax rate rises with the level of income. This situation is illustrated in Panel A of **Figure 2.5** as a nonlinear tax schedule. Income levels are assumed to vary each year between low and high. If the firm uses hedging strategies to reduce the volatility in income, the tax liability of that more stable income level is lower than the average of the taxes paid without hedging. Risk management, therefore, can reduce the tax burden if the tax schedule is progressive.

Panel B of Figure 2.5 illustrates the case where the probability distribution of net income contains a material chance of loss for the year if the firm conducts no hedging activity. Suppose that the firm has tax loss carryforwards or foreign tax credits from previous years that are about to expire. The problem is that if the firm has a bad year and does not record a profit, those tax benefits will expire worthless. A hedging strategy could conceivably be designed to tighten the probability distribution on net income to reduce dramatically the probability of subzero profitability. Notice that the mean of the distribution with hedging is shifted to the left, reflecting the cost of the risk-containment program. Those costs might be the premiums on a package of options to protect the firm from unexpectedly higher costs of production and financing. The idea is that, although expected pretax income is lower, expected after-tax income could be higher because of the greater probability of capturing the tax benefits.

Next, suppose that bankruptcy costs exist, in the sense that reducing the probability of financial distress is valued by the various stakeholders in the firm beyond the shareholders—the employees, the customers, the suppliers.

---

[5]See Smith and Stulz (1985).

Figure 2.5. Value Added from Risk Management

A. With Nonlinear Tax Schedule

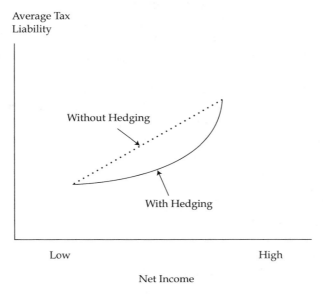

B. With a Material Chance of Loss

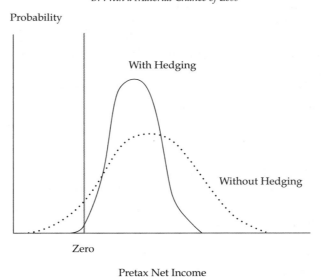

The value of employee training, the pricing of warranties and long-term service contracts, and the ability to obtain favorable delivery contracts with suppliers depend on the perceived financial well-being of the firm. These positive "externalities" offset to some degree the costs of hedging, but these benefits would only accrue to the shareholders to the extent that the firm communicates its commitment to risk reduction to these other stakeholders.

In the theoretical M&M world, investors hold well-diversified portfolios. In reality, some investors are not at all well-diversified, either by circumstance or by intent. Examples include owners of family businesses, entrepreneurs, and managers taking firms private by means of a leveraged buyout. In these situations, risk management at the level of the firm can substitute for portfolio diversification at the level of the individual investor.

This discussion suggests that derivatives can play a value-adding role in corporate risk management when the strict M&M assumptions are violated. But these applications do not constitute a *normative theory* of financial risk management. The open question is: What *should* a firm's objective be with regard to hedging? Froot, Scharfstein, and Stein (1993, 1994) provide one answer. The objective, they argue, should be to ensure that the firm has cash available to make good investments. They base this prescription on the observation that firms finance most investments from internally generated funds. Firms also tend to trim their capital budgets if there is a cash shortfall, rather than accessing more expensive external debt and equity markets. This practice can lead to a less-than-optimal level of investment when adverse interest rate, exchange rate, or commodity price movements reduce cash flows below a critical level. The proper goal for risk management, therefore, is not simply to eliminate or reduce risk in general. Instead, it is to align the supply of internally generated funds with investment needs.

Stulz (1996) argues along similar lines to Froot, Scharfstein, and Stein and concludes that the objective for corporate risk management should be to make financial distress very unlikely, thereby preserving the firm's ability to fulfill its investment strategy. The problem, essentially, is to eliminate the "lower-tail" outcomes on the probability distribution of the firm's profits. In his view, risk management is a substitute for equity capital because it allows the firm to increase its debt capacity. Therefore, the strategy for risk management should be set jointly with capital structure decisions.

Evidence on Market Practice

A main source of our current understanding about corporate risk management practices is a series of surveys of U.S. nonfinancial firms conducted by the Wharton School of the University of Pennsylvania. The first survey in 1994 was conducted in conjunction with Chase Manhattan Bank—Bodnar, Hayt, Marston, and Smithson (1995). The second two, in 1995 and 1998, were sponsored by the Canadian Imperial Bank of Commerce—Bodnar, Hayt, and Marston (1996, 1998).

Some clear patterns and consistent results about risk management practices emerge from these surveys.

- Derivatives are not universally used by nonfinancial firms. Only in the 1998 survey did the proportion of firms responding that they use derivatives (meaning options, futures, forwards, and swaps) reach one-half. In the 1994 survey, the subsample of users was just 35 percent (183 of 530). That figure rose to 41 percent (142 of 350) in 1995 and to 50 percent (200 of 399) in 1998.

- Among those firms that reported not using derivatives, the most common explanation was insufficient exposure. Other reasons were that the exposures were managed by other means, the costs of hedging exceeded the expected benefits, and they were concerned about perceptions of derivative use. The last reason is notable. Twenty-five percent of the firms not using derivatives in the 1998 survey cited concerns about the perceptions of derivative use as the first or second reason for not using external hedging methods. But note that "not using derivatives" does not mean "not actively managing risk." In theory, at least, all derivatives can be replicated by positions in other assets and liabilities. Some of the "other means" could involve what we have called internal hedging.

- Derivative use varies dramatically with firm size. For instance, in the 1998 survey, 83 percent of the firms designated as "large" reported use of derivatives. That figure dropped to 45 percent for medium-sized firms and to only 12 percent for small firms. The same pattern was observed by Dolde (1993) in an earlier survey of 244 of the Fortune 500 companies. This positive correlation between firm size and derivative use is consistent with the notion of fixed costs. A considerable up-front investment in human and technological resources seems to deter smaller firms from using external hedging methods. Larger firms can amortize those costs over more or larger transactions.

- Derivative use differs by industry type. In 1998, 68 percent of primary products firms, 48 percent of manufacturing firms, and 42 percent of service firms reported use of derivatives. This finding is not surprising. Firms producing primary products are more likely than service firms to have exposure to a commodity that has an organized futures market. Moving up the learning curve by managing one type of exposure, often starting with currency or commodity price risk, should enable the firm to use derivatives with other sources of risk.

- Derivative use also differs by the type of risk. Of the 1998 subsample that used derivatives, 83 percent used them to manage FX risk, 76 percent for interest rate risk, 56 percent for commodity price risk, and 34 percent for equity price risk. Again, this finding is not surprising. FX risk is probably the most visible and easiest to measure exposure facing the typical firm having international operations.
- The most commonly used products follow the type of risk being managed. Forward contracts were the derivative of choice for FX risk management, swaps for interest rate risk management, futures contracts for commodity risk, and OTC options for equity risk. This pattern has its roots in the history of derivatives. Futures markets started with commodity contracts many years ago and introduced FX and interest rate contracts only in the 1970s, when market volatility became significant. Swaps can be interpreted as multiperiod forward contracts. Their widespread use with interest rate risk parallels the longer time frame for exposures.
- With regard to FX exposure, firms are more inclined to hedge on-balance-sheet than off-balance-sheet commitments (in the 1998 survey, an average of 49 percent of on-balance-sheet commitments were hedged, compared with 23 percent of off-balance-sheet commitments) and more inclined to hedge anticipated transactions occurring within one year than those beyond one year (42 percent and 16 percent, respectively). Also, firms tend to hedge cash repatriations (40 percent) more than translation of foreign accounts (12 percent). It is noteworthy that firms rarely hedge more than 50 percent of their exposures. In practice, risk reduction is more the norm than risk elimination.
- In managing interest rate risk, nonfinancial firms more commonly swap from floating-rate to fixed-rate exposures than from fixed to floating. About half of the firms using derivatives in the 1998 survey reported that they sometimes (as opposed to frequently or never) fixed rates or spreads in advance of a debt issuance (50 percent) and attempted to reduce the cost of borrowed funds based on a market rate view (48 percent).
- Many firms that use derivatives alter the size and timing of their FX and interest rate hedges based on a market view. About 5–10 percent in the 1998 survey acknowledged that this modification is done frequently, and 50–60 percent said they do it sometimes. Moreover, about one-third admitted to frequently or sometimes actively taking positions in FX and interest rates based on their market view. This finding illustrates the fine line between hedging and speculation. Hedging less of an exposure can accomplish the same result as taking a view outright and speculating.

- Options are used less frequently than forwards in FX risk management, less than swaps in interest rate risk management, and less than futures in commodity risk management. Overall, the majority (about two-thirds) of all firms surveyed eschew the use of options. The 1995 survey explicitly sought evidence about the choice between options and forwards/futures in managing currency risk. Forwards and futures were deemed much more important for contractual exposures than options were (86 percent and 7 percent, respectively) and for anticipated transactions within one year (66 percent and 30 percent, respectively). Options, however, were deemed more important for anticipated transactions beyond one year (51 percent and 43 percent) and for competitive and economic exposures (67 percent and 24 percent).

- Use of so-called exotic, or nonstandard, options is not commonplace but not rare either. Although 68 percent of the derivative-using firms in the 1998 survey reported having bought or sold options of any variety, 19 percent used average rate options and 13 percent used barrier options. Average rate contracts (whereby payoffs are determined by some average of prices or rates rather than by the price or rate on a single date) were used more for commodities and FX exposures than for interest rate risk. Barrier options (whereby the contract is either extinguished or only becomes effective if a certain price or rate level is attained) were used mostly with currency risk. FX seems to provide the most popular setting for innovations in derivatives. Basket options (whereby the payoff depends on some group of underlying product prices or rates) and contingent premium options (whereby the premium is deferred or depends on some event) were used more in FX risk management than with commodities or interest rates.

- Most firms using derivatives have a documented policy governing their use and make regular reports to the board of directors (86 percent in the 1998 survey). But the remaining 14 percent (an amount consistent with the earlier surveys) had no written policy or specific reporting cycle.

- A significant change occurred between 1995 and 1998 regarding how firms value their outstanding derivative positions in their periodic financial reports. Before 1995, the most common method by far was to use valuations provided by the originating dealer. More recently, the most common method has become a source within the company. This shift to internal pricing sources indicates the growing sophistication among end-users and the expanded availability of market data for use with low-cost spreadsheet models.

- Many firms using derivatives regard risk management, at least implicitly, as a profit center. In the 1998 survey, firms were asked about their philosophy regarding how the risk management function is evaluated. Choices were "reduced volatility relative to a benchmark" (selected by 40 percent of the derivative users), "increased profit or reduced costs relative to a benchmark" (22 percent), "absolute profit/loss" (18 percent), and "risk-adjusted performance—profits or savings adjusted for volatility" (21 percent). The authors of the survey report conclude that the second and third choices, representing 40 percent of users, illustrated philosophies that "provide incentives for risk managers to take positions that may ultimately increase the total riskiness of the firm."

Surveys, of course, are not audits of market practice. Surely, some respondents feel inclined to give what they think are the "right" answers to the questions that are asked. Some respondents no doubt are merely guessing in answering some questions (e.g., the percentage of exposures to various types of risks hedged with derivatives). Nevertheless, the main results of these surveys are consistent across time and with other published results.

In addition to this descriptive evidence on corporate risk management practices, some recent empirical research in the academic literature is shedding further light on the use of derivatives. A particularly interesting study is by Gay and Nam (1998). They find evidence to support the underinvestment hypothesis that emerges from the work by Froot, Scharfstein, and Stein discussed previously. Gay and Nam find that firms are more inclined to use derivatives when they have greater investment opportunities and when they have relatively lower cash balances. In addition, they find a negative relationship between the correlation of the firm's internally generated funds with its investment outlays and the use of derivatives. The more correlated the internal funds and investment outlays, the less derivatives are used. That finding implies that firms hedge less when they are already internally hedged, in that cash flows are higher when investment needs are higher and vice versa. On the other hand, firms are more inclined to use derivatives when a weaker correlation exists between internal funds and investment outlays.

Tufano (1996, 1998) takes a different approach to risk management issues. He examines the circumstances when conflicts might arise between the interests of corporate managers and shareholders. Some notable results emerge from his landmark study of hedging practices in the gold mining industry. He examines a number of firms that hedge the price of their future gold sales to varying degrees. The only systematic determinants of the hedge ratio (the proportion of future production that is hedged) turn out to be the percentage of total shares outstanding that are owned by managers and the particular type of managerial compensation scheme. One result is that the greater the percentage of shares owned by managers, the more the firm hedges. A second result is that when stock options are more important in overall management compensation, the amount of hedging is lower. Both results are consistent with managers' making decisions to maximize their own utility functions to the detriment of shareholders who would not necessarily prefer that degree of risk reduction. The astute analyst will look for suboptimal hedging policies that may be linked to the presence or absence of a significant employee stock option plan.

Summary

Actions taken that modify the risk–reward relationship of the initial position can be classified as hedging, speculation, or arbitrage. Although no one would disapprove of exploiting a profitable arbitrage opportunity, the decision to reduce the level of risk by hedging or to increase the risk level by speculation is inherently a difficult one to make and can be controversial. How risk is measured, in whose interest it is managed, and what identified objective function is maximized affect risk management decisions. Sorting these decisions out, in theory as well as in practice, is not an easy task.

Theoretical justifications for the use of derivatives to reduce risk are relatively easy to find when the assumptions that drive the classic M&M irrelevancy results are relaxed. Derivatives add value to the firm when they reduce expected tax obligations and the probability of costly financial distress and when they substitute for diversification that cannot be carried out directly by owners. Recent academic work addresses directly what the role of corporate risk management should be—to ensure that the firm can make profitable investments, which means having cash from internal sources to fund the capital budget and having protection from events that would upset the investment strategy.

The evidence of risk management practices in the marketplace indicates that many firms do not have formal risk management policies and practices but rather make case-by-case decisions. Some firms may carefully manage foreign exchange, interest rate, and commodity price risk by looking at such issues as cash flows, but others are basing their hedge ratios on their views of future market conditions. And although some firms may be practicing true hedging, others are deliberately choosing when to hedge and when not to hedge based on their market views and are thus engaging in a form of speculation that concerns financial analysts.

3. Corporate Risk Management: The Financial Analyst's Challenge

Corporate risk management decisions are fundamentally decisions about risk and reward—decisions that clearly affect a firm's financial health. As a result, these risk management decisions are (or should be) of concern to financial analysts. But until the Financial Accounting Standards Board (FASB) released Statement of Financial Accounting Standards (SFAS) No. 133, *Accounting for Derivative Instruments and Hedging Activities*—which is effective for all fiscal quarters for all fiscal years beginning after June 15, 2000—analysts were often completely in the dark.

The driving force behind the need for a new standard was incompleteness and inconsistency in existing standards. Authoritative standards existed for only subsets of the derivatives commonly used to manage risk. Moreover, different rules were applied to different instruments and different sources of risk, even when they were functional equivalents from the perspective of the risk manager.

Although clarification and harmonization of accounting rules were inevitable, the "derivative debacles" of 1994 brought a sense of urgency to the process. A number of firms suffered dramatic and highly publicized losses on positions in derivatives when interest rates rose in the spring of 1994 following the tightening of monetary policy by the U.S. Federal Reserve. These losses were not simply the losses to be expected on one leg of a hedged position. The losses reflected changes in the market values of positions that were clearly outside the scope of risk reduction via hedging and in the realm of outright speculation.

The FASB had been working since 1986 to develop a comprehensive standard for hedge accounting and the use of derivatives, but after the derivative debacles, the U.S. Securities and Exchange Commission (SEC), among others, called for more disclosure of derivative positions in financial statements. So, in June of 1996, the FASB released an exposure draft that after two years of comments, testimony, and much controversy became the core of SFAS No. 133.

Accounting for Derivatives before SFAS No. 133

The greatest problem in accounting for derivatives and risk management prior to SFAS No. 133 was incomplete and inconsistent guidance. Given the lack of authoritative rulings, accountants had to rely on analogies to and interpretations of existing literature, and sometimes guesswork. SFAS No. 52, *Foreign Currency Translation*, and SFAS No. 80, *Accounting for Futures Contracts*, specifically address only a limited set of products and strategies. To supplement those statements, accountants also used several publications of the FASB's Emerging Issues Task Force (EITF). Although EITF statements of issues do not carry the weight of formal FASB statements, they do provide guidance in particular situations. For example, EITF Issue No. 84-7 discusses accounting for the termination of an interest rate swap.

Hedge Accounting. A key concern in accounting for derivatives has been whether hedge accounting applies. If it does not apply, the position has to be marked to market and has to have changes in value (realized or not) run through the income statement, similar to how a speculative or unhedged transaction would be treated. If hedge accounting applies, gains and losses on the position are deferred until the underlying transaction and the hedge are closed out. The three general criteria for hedge accounting prior to SFAS No. 133 were *designation* (naming the derivative position as a hedge when it was established), *risk reduction* (identifying the presence of some material exposure to an uncertain price or rate movement that the derivative position was expected to reduce), and *effectiveness* (establishing that the derivative could reasonably be expected to achieve its purpose of reducing risk).

Suppose that in fiscal year 1995 a shoe manufacturer that had all of its expenses denominated in U.S. dollars (USD) received a contract to deliver a shipment of shoes to a Canadian retail chain in its fiscal year 1996; the quantity to be shipped and the price in Canadian dollars (CAD) were set when the contract was entered. An obvious strategy for the manufacturer to reduce its exposure to weakness in CAD would have been to commit to sell the CAD it would receive in fiscal year 1996 on a forward basis for a set amount of USD. If this foreign exchange (FX) forward contract had been treated as a hedge, any unrealized gains or losses on the contract at year-end would have been deferred until the next year. At that time, the realized gain or loss when the FX forward contract was settled would have been combined with the sale of the CAD payment when it was received. The effect would have been to lock in a value in USD for the combined FX and shoe transaction for 1996, thus eliminating any impact on financial statements for 1995. But if hedge accounting had not applied (suppose that the sale was not contractual but reflected the hoped-for outcome of an appearance at a

Toronto trade show), the mark-to-market value of the FX forward contract would have flowed through the income statement for 1995.

Forwards and Futures. SFAS No. 52 covers the use of foreign currency forward and futures contracts and currency swaps. According to SFAS No. 52, FX risk is to be identified and measured on a transaction-by-transaction basis and not on the aggregate level of the enterprise as a whole. But because only exposures to firm commitments qualify for hedge accounting treatment, forwards and futures that aim to reduce the FX risk on anticipated (but not yet firmly committed) transactions have to be marked to market and have changes in value reported in the current income statement. Note that earnings volatility is greater in the current year if the change in mark-to-market value is deferred until the transaction is consummated in the next fiscal year.

SFAS No. 80 covers futures contracts other than those for managing currency risk. These primarily are interest rate and commodity futures. In contrast to the transaction-specific treatment of FX risk in SFAS No. 52, interest rate and commodity price risks governed by SFAS No. 80 are identified and measured on an enterprise basis. That is, a futures contract designated as a hedge has to be expected to reduce interest rate or commodity price risk at the level of the firm (or at least the business unit) and not just on a particular transaction. This standard is more challenging than it may seem at first, especially for interest rate risk in a nonfinancial firm. The inherent difficulty is identifying and measuring the sensitivity of cash flows from operations based on changes in interest rates. That sensitivity can arise from a number of macroeconomic sources—anticipated inflation, the business cycle, and FX rate fluctuations. In principle, the risk manager has to quantify the correlations of those macroeconomic variables that determine the level of operating cash flows with the level of interest rates that determine the firm's cost of borrowed funds.

Even though enterprise risk is reduced by a hedge transaction under SFAS No. 80, the derivative serving as the hedge has to be assigned to a particular asset, liability, or transaction. Unlike under SFAS No. 52, anticipated transactions as well as firm commitments affecting interest rate and commodity price risk qualify for hedge accounting; however, anticipated transactions have to be deemed to be "probable" and have identified terms and characteristics. This effectiveness criterion for hedge accounting is based on a high correlation between changes in the value of the futures contract and the designated underlying asset, liability, or transaction. Although the actual correlation has to be monitored regularly, SFAS No. 80 is silent on how correlation is to be measured and what constitutes "high" correlation. In practice, many firms have adopted the 80–120 rule, whereby the change in the derivative has to be within 80 percent and 120 percent of the change in the underlying position.[1]

Swaps and Options. Although SFAS No. 52 and SFAS No. 80 address a significant set of derivative instruments used in managing risk, they provide no authoritative guidance concerning plain-vanilla swaps or options—let alone guidance on the more "exotic" derivative varieties that have been developed in recent years—even though swaps and options are among the most widely used derivatives in risk management. The financial accounting for these products has developed mainly by analogy to SFAS Nos. 52 and 80 and in line with several EITF issues.

Interest rate swaps effectively convert a floating-rate debt security to a fixed-rate obligation, or vice versa from a fixed rate to a floating rate. The notion of "synthetic alteration," introduced in EITF Issue No. 84-36, emerged as the standard way of accounting for swap contracts. The idea is that if a combination of securities and derivatives creates a sequence of cash flows equivalent to another security, the comparable position should have the same accounting treatment. For example, consider a firm that issues a floating-rate note (FRN) that pays a semiannual coupon interest rate set at six-month LIBOR (the London Interbank Offered Rate) plus 0.25 percent. An interest rate swap to receive six-month LIBOR and pay a fixed rate of 6 percent transforms that FRN into a synthetic 6.25 percent fixed-rate liability, as shown in **Figure 3.1**. This example assumes that the payment frequencies, maturity dates, day-count conventions, and principal amounts on the FRN and the swap are the same.

In practice, synthetic alteration led accountants to conclude that the FRN/swap combination is to be accounted for in the same manner as a straight fixed-rate note. For the issuer, the FRN is carried on the balance sheet in the same manner as if the firm had issued the fixed-rate note. The interest payments on the FRN and the net settlements on the swap flow through interest expense together. The fair value of the swap is reported only in the footnotes, aggregated with other derivatives. Following SFAS No. 80, the swap has to be properly designated and the floating rates on the swap and the FRN have to be highly correlated. For example, if the FRN pays coupon interest tied to an index of commercial paper rates, the firm has to establish that LIBOR and the commercial paper index are highly correlated.

In contrast to the guidance in SFAS No. 80, an interest rate swap accounted for using the principle of synthetic alteration does not have to reduce the interest rate risk of the enterprise. For example, consider a firm that has assets

---

[1]See Kawaller and Koch (2000) for further discussion of the effectiveness criterion.

Figure 3.1. Conversion of FRN into a Synthetic Fixed-Rate Note

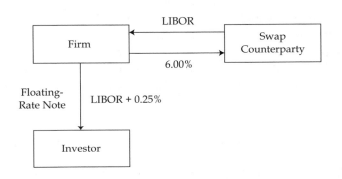

A. FRN/Swap Combination

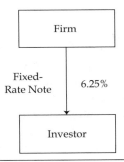

B. Straight Fixed-Rate Note

generating income flows that are highly correlated with short-term interest rates. If the firm issues an FRN to finance the acquisition of those assets, it will be internally hedged against interest rate volatility—operating income and interest expense will rise and fall together. Suppose further that the firm swaps that FRN for a synthetic fixed rate, as shown in Figure 3.1. That swap has actually introduced interest rate risk to the enterprise. Nevertheless, the swap qualifies for hedge accounting treatment because overall interest rate risk reduction is not a criterion in this situation. As will be shown later, one of the curiosities of SFAS No. 133 is that this circumstance not only continues but is also extended to all derivatives. Under the new rules of SFAS No. 133, risk reduction on an enterprise basis is no longer a requirement for hedge accounting treatment.

Perhaps the most important aspect of the accounting for options that developed by analogy to the statements preceding SFAS No. 133 was that only purchased options could qualify as a hedge. Written options, both calls and puts, were deemed to be speculative by nature because of their "unlimited" potential losses.[2] The premium received for writing the option was not recorded as income until the contract expired or was exercised. Then, the premium was offset by any payment made to the buyer of the option.

The accounting for purchased options illustrates some of the inconsistency in the pre-SFAS No. 133 environment. Recall that in SFAS No. 52, FX futures and forwards qualify for hedge accounting only if the underlying exposure is from a firm commitment. EITF Issue No. 90-17, however, states that an option to buy a certain amount of a foreign currency at a set exchange rate can be used to hedge an anticipated transaction.

Disclosure Requirements. Disclosure requirements prior to SFAS No. 133 were generally guided by SFAS No. 119, *Disclosure about Derivative Financial Instruments and Fair Value of Financial Instruments*. SFAS No. 119 added to and amended two other statements (SFAS No. 105, *Disclosure of Information about Financial Instruments with Off-Balance-Sheet Risk and Financial Instruments with Concentrations of Credit Risk,* and SFAS No. 107, *Disclosures about Fair Value of Financial Instruments*) that emerged from the FASB project on financial instruments, which started in 1986. Because derivative use and the complexity of the products were increasing rapidly throughout this time period, the analyst community started demanding increased corporate disclosure of positions, strategy, and risk.

SFAS No. 119 separates derivative activity by purpose—for trading and for other than trading. This separation was an attempt to get at the important, but sometimes difficult, distinction between speculating and hedging. Under SFAS No. 119, the average fair value of traded derivatives has to be reported either in the body of the financial statements or in notes, along with gains and losses by the type of instrument. Derivatives held for purposes other than trading are presumably used to manage risk. New in SFAS No. 119 were requirements that firms disclose their objectives and strategies, how and when they would recognize gains and losses on their derivatives, and when anticipated transactions were expected to occur.

SFAS No. 119 also recommends (but, notably, does not require) that firms disclose quantitative information about the market risks associated with their

---

[2]The maximum loss on a written put option is limited to its strike price, less the premium received, because the price of the underlying instrument will not go below zero. But the asymmetry of the position (the gain is limited to the premium received) disqualifies it from hedge treatment.

derivative positions. The recommended methods of disclosing these data are sensitivity analysis, tables, and a summary value-at-risk (VAR) statistic.[3]

The Derivative Debacles of 1994

Perhaps the ultimate nightmare for a financial analyst is discovering that the firm he or she thought was so well understood and conservatively managed is an aggressive hedge fund in disguise. The events surrounding Gibson Greetings, a producer of greeting cards and gift wrapping paper, in the early 1990s present a classic example of this scenario. But Gibson was not the only firm that was aggressively taking positions in structured derivatives. Procter & Gamble (P&G) also reported a major loss on positions in derivatives in the spring of 1994. But P&G was able to absorb its announced $157 million pretax write-off to earnings without major financial impact. Even if P&G had not been able to recoup most of the losses from Bankers Trust, the counterparty to its swap transactions, the ultimate outcome probably would have been viewed by P&G's management as more of a public relations problem than a fiscal disaster. Gibson Greetings, however, suffered losses on its positions in derivatives (before its own settlement with Bankers Trust) that amounted to a significant percentage of its annual net income.

Consider the plight of a financial analyst attempting to understand the risks and the potential reward of an investment in Gibson Greetings in early 1993. **Table 3.1** provides some relevant data. The major concern to the analyst would have seemed to be the drop in net income in 1992. The adverse change was attributed in part to the Chapter 11 filing by Phar-Mor, a retail drugstore chain that had been Gibson's major customer. Gibson wrote off more than $16 million in receivables from Phar-Mor. The analyst facing these results very likely would have focused on the firm's new marketing and distribution strategies vis-à-vis its competitors.

Table 3.1. Relevant Financial Data for Gibson Greetings, 1989–92
(thousands)

Year	Net Sales	Net Income	Long-Term Debt
1989	$463,290	$42,369	$30,425
1990	511,211	39,800	21,755
1991	522,211	41,884	71,079
1992	484,118	6,536	70,175

[3]VAR is a measure of the dollar amount of loss over a certain time period subject to a specified degree of statistical confidence.

The analyst also would have noticed the jump in long-term debt that occurred in 1991. Gibson Greetings privately placed $50 million of senior notes in May of 1991 to reduce short-term debt. The notes had a fixed coupon of 9.33 percent and serial maturities from 1995 through 2001. Some of these notes were modified by interest rate swaps during 1991 and 1992. The firm disclosed its derivative positions and risk management strategy in its 1992 annual report using the following language:

> The Company periodically enters into interest rate swap agreements with the intent to manage the interest rate sensitivity of portions of its debt. At December 31, 1992, the Company had four outstanding interest rate swap agreements with a total notional principal amount of $67,200,000. Two of the agreements, with terms similar to the related bonds, effectively change the Company's interest rate on $3,600,000 of industrial revenue bonds to 6.67 percent through February 1998. The other two agreements, the original terms of which were five years and four and one-half years, effectively change the Company's interest rate on $30,000,000 of senior notes to 5.41 percent through April 1993 and 5.44 percent through October 1993 and thereafter to a floating-rate obligation adjusted semi-annually through October 1997. The estimated cost to terminate the Company's swap portfolio would be $775,000 at December 31, 1992. (Chew 1996, pp. 69–70)

The financial analyst reading this statement could quite reasonably have concluded that these were plain-vanilla, fixed versus floating, interest rate swaps that were used to "manage the interest rate sensitivity of portions of its debt." To manage the interest sensitivity of the senior notes, the firm, it would seem, had entered into swaps to receive a fixed rate and to pay a floating rate (e.g., LIBOR). Given the upward slope to yield curves that prevailed in the market at that time, a receive-fixed swap would have generated initial cash receipts that could have lowered the firm's cost of funds to the indicated levels. The swaps also would have converted the debt to a floating-rate obligation for the remainder of the five-year term of the swap.

The analyst, in assessing the impact of these derivative transactions, might have been concerned that a greeting card company had converted fixed-rate debt to floating-rate obligations. Usually, locking in the cost of borrowed funds—as opposed to acquiring a floating-rate cost of funds—is viewed as a risk-reducing strategy. Thus, it might have appeared that Gibson had exposed itself to unexpectedly higher interest rates in the market in the following years.

What the analyst would have had absolutely no way of knowing from this disclosure was that this was not a plain-vanilla swap at all. It was, in fact, a structured swap having an innovative (to be generous) floating-rate structure. On October 1, 1992, Gibson Greetings entered a five-year, 5.50 percent, $30,000,000 receive-fixed "ratio" swap with Bankers Trust. Instead of paying six-month LIBOR on the swap, as would be the case with a plain-vanilla design, Gibson was obligated to pay LIBOR[2] divided by 6 percent. This arrangement is illustrated in **Figure 3.2**.

Figure 3.2. Gibson Greetings "Ratio" Swap

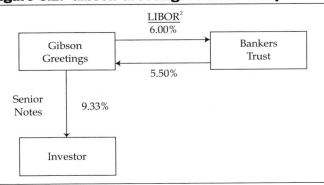

Some other terms of this swap are significant if one is to understand the statement in the 1992 annual report. For the first year of the swap, six-month LIBOR was set at 3.08 percent between October 1992 and April 1993 and at 3.37 percent from April to October 1993. Therefore, for the initial six months, Gibson was scheduled to receive a net payment of 3.92 percent:

$$5.50\% - \frac{(3.08\%)^2}{6.00\%} = 5.50\% - 1.58\%$$
$$= 3.92\%.$$

The dollar payment is calculated by multiplying this net rate payment by the notional principal of $30,000,000 and then times one-half because the payments were semiannual. The 9.33 percent coupon rate on the underlying senior notes less the locked-in receipt of 3.92 percent on the swap gives the adjusted cost of funds identified in the annual report of 5.41 percent.

The calculation of the net rate for the second six months is even more complicated. Gibson was scheduled to receive a net settlement rate of 3.61 percent on the swap, based on the preset level of 3.37 percent for LIBOR:

$$5.50\% - \frac{(3.37\%)^2}{6.00\%} = 5.50\% - 1.89\%$$
$$= 3.61\%.$$

The fixed coupon of 9.33 percent on the notes less this net receipt on the swap of 3.61 percent equals an interest cost of 5.72 percent, which, apparently, is where the second $30,000,000 swap enters. On it, Gibson was to receive 0.28 percent as long as the current level of six-month LIBOR was above the level of LIBOR six months beforehand less 0.15 percent, although the precise terms of this deal are difficult to determine from available documents. Note that 5.72 percent less 0.28 percent would equal the rate of 5.44 percent given in the annual report.

The relevant concern is that the statement in the 1992 annual report that "two agreements . . . effectively change . . . the Company's interest rate . . . to a floating-rate obligation" is misleading, to say the least. Moreover, these turned out not to be merely "one-off" ventures into the world of exotic derivatives. Instead, they led to a series of deals with compelling names, such as "the spread lock," "the knock-out call option," "the time swap," and "the wedding band."[4] The exact terms of the series of transactions were not revealed, but the firm's obligations apparently grew rapidly as interest rates rose. The division of LIBOR[2] by 6.00 percent would have given a rate of 8.17 percent with LIBOR at 7.00 percent and 10.67 percent with LIBOR at 8.00 percent. Gibson Greetings ended up filing an 8-K report with the SEC in April of 1994 announcing that it had taken a charge against first-quarter earnings in the amount of $16.7 million for losses on derivatives, in addition to a $3 million charge taken a month earlier.

About the same time the Gibson Greetings fiasco was becoming public, Procter & Gamble announced its $157 million loss on two swaps. That announcement was followed by similar revelations from Federated Paper Board ($11 million) and Air Products & Chemicals ($122 million). Some common threads connect these events. The deals, typically, were complex swap agreements and involved some type of leverage. Moreover, the accounting practice of synthetic alteration was deemed to allow the swaps to be combined with underlying notes and not to be marked to market as separate instruments. The settlement cash flows on the swaps were simply adjustments to the interest income or expense on the underlying notes. The key problem with this reporting is that an analyst, knowing only the fixed rates and notional principals on the swaps, would have had no sense of the actual market risks involved.

Some of the derivative deals that "blew up" in 1994 contained embedded written options. For example, Procter & Gamble effectively wrote put options on 5-year and 30-year Treasury securities in one of its swaps with Bankers Trust. The "premium" received by P&G for selling the options showed up as a lower floating rate to be paid (P&G was the receiver of the fixed rate and payer of the floating rate). The payment to Bankers Trust if the options turned out to be in the money (which, of course, they did) showed up as an addition to the floating rate. The extraordinary leverage in the deal resulted in approximately a $100 million loss on a $200 million notional principal swap.[5]

These dramatic losses revealed in no uncertain terms the inadequacies of existing accounting rules for derivatives. According to generally accepted

---

[4]See Overdahl and Schachter (1995) or Chew for descriptions of these transactions.

[5]See Smith (1997) for further analysis of this transaction.

accounting principles (GAAP) at the time, a written option did not qualify for hedge accounting and had to be marked to market. But leveraged swaps containing functionally equivalent written options fell through the gaps in GAAP! Firms that never would have considered writing (selling) stand-alone uncovered options on an exchange or over the counter were perfectly willing to write comparable options that were embedded in a swap with a bank counterparty. These swaps merely "synthetically altered" some underlying note that was carried at book value on the balance sheet. These abuses to the spirit of hedge accounting left the standard setters at the FASB with little alternative: The rules had to be changed to provide users of financial statements with greater transparency concerning the risk of derivative positions.

The Genesis of SFAS No. 133

In 1986, the FASB embarked on a financial instruments project that had as one of its objectives the development of a comprehensive standard for hedge accounting and the use of derivatives. Although the project continues, the release of SFAS No. 133 in June of 1998 has provided the most comprehensive change to date in the reporting of risk management activities.

Accounting for Derivatives under SFAS No. 133. SFAS No. 133 introduces major changes in the way derivatives are treated in financial statements. Henceforth, nearly all derivatives will be carried on the balance sheet at their fair market values. Previously, most derivatives were carried off balance sheet and reported only in footnotes to the financial statements. Depending on the reason for holding the derivative position and the position's effectiveness in the firm's risk management strategy, changes in the position's fair value will now be recorded either in the income statement or in a component of equity known as *other comprehensive income*.

Perhaps the most significant change implemented by SFAS No. 133 is a movement away from a focus on accounting for particular derivative instruments and on the source of risk (e.g., futures contracts hedging FX risk) and toward a focus on the types of risk being managed. Three types of risk are identified in SFAS No. 133: (1) exposure to changes in the *fair value* of assets or liabilities already on the balance sheet or to a firm commitment the enterprise has made; (2) exposure to changes in *cash flows* associated with assets or liabilities or anticipated future transactions; and (3) exposure to changes in *foreign exchange rates* that affect the value of firm commitments, forecasted transactions, available-for-sale debt securities, and the net investment in foreign operations. Positions in derivatives to manage these exposures are referred to, respectively, as fair-value hedges, cash flow hedges, and hedges of net investment in foreign operations.

The Battle over the Exposure Draft. In June of 1996, the FASB released its exposure draft, "Accounting for Derivatives and Similar Financial Instruments and for Hedging Activities." It sparked much discussion and controversy, which should not come as a shock. The FASB has proposed a number of controversial changes to accounting standards in recent years, and not surprisingly, opposition to the changes has usually emerged from those industries most affected by the proposals. In the 1980s, a major controversy erupted over accounting for retiree health benefits. At that time, the big manufacturing firms were aligned in opposition to the FASB's proposals for change. In the 1990s, the FASB issued an exposure draft on accounting for employee stock options. This exposure draft was opposed (somewhat successfully in this case) by high-tech firms that claimed that having to treat the value of stock options granted to employees as a current expense would be a disaster (to their share prices).[6]

In the case of the FASB's exposure draft on accounting for derivatives, the focused opposition came from financial institutions, notably large commercial banks that were not only end-users of derivatives but also producers and marketers of these instruments. In August of 1997, the FASB released a revised draft that necessitated a second round of comments. Well over 100 responses to the draft were received at the FASB during the two formal comment periods.

A number of changes were made to the proposal as a result of the comments and discussions at FASB-sponsored forums. Many of these changes were clarifications of the following questions:

* What exactly is a derivative in the context of the statement?
* What is a hybrid instrument containing an embedded derivative?
* What happens when a hedge position is closed or the underlying exposure is terminated?
* How is the effectiveness of a hedge to be measured?

The proposed accounting for hybrids was important to investment firms because the exposure draft called for bifurcating the embedded derivative and the host instrument. This requirement would mean that firms owning or issuing structured notes might have to extract the embedded forward or option contracts and report them as separate derivatives (i.e., at fair value)

---

[6]On a more technical level, the ensuing discussion revealed some difficulties in measuring the market value of employee stock options. The assumptions behind typical option-valuation models (e.g., the Black–Scholes model) do not conform to the terms of nontraded, long-term contingent claims when, for example, managerial decisions can affect the interim and ultimate value of the underlying security and the very exercise of the options dilutes the value of the stock.

with gains and losses flowing directly through the income statement each reporting period. Ultimately, the FASB exempted structured notes acquired prior to January 1, 1998, and instruments held in a trading portfolio from the new standard (because changes in fair value on these instruments already flow through the income statement).

Although the FASB remained resolute in its determination to have all derivatives recognized at fair value on the balance sheet, it compromised on many points. A good example is the partial retreat on written options, overturning the long-standing position that only purchased options qualify for hedge accounting. The FASB decided to allow net written options to be designated as hedging instruments when the hedged item is an already owned long-option position.

Commercial banks' opposition to the exposure draft reflected their perspective as major end-users as well as producers and marketers of derivatives. One of their overriding concerns was that there might be less derivative activity under the proposed rules. Compliance costs undoubtedly would go up, mostly because the effectiveness of hedges would have to be monitored and accounted for. Also, volatility of some components of the financial statement surely would go up. This volatility would show up in the income statement or in equity (i.e., the other comprehensive income component), depending on the effectiveness of the hedge in reducing the identified risk. In theory, volatility in earnings per share would increase only to the extent that a hedge is *not* effective in reducing risk. The importance and relevance of this concern for earnings stability ultimately comes down to how readers of financial statements understand and interpret earnings volatility. Understanding and interpretation are important parts of the *raison d'être* of this (and other) efforts to explain SFAS No. 133.

Summary

There is no question that entering the mid-1990s a new accounting standard dealing with derivatives, hedging, and risk management was needed. Existing guidance—largely from SFAS No. 52, SFAS No. 80, and several EITF issues—was inconsistent and incomplete. SFAS No. 52 identifies exposures to risk on a transactional basis; SFAS No. 80, on an enterprise basis. The former limits hedge accounting to firm commitments only; the latter expands hedging treatment to transactions that are sufficiently "probable." Swaps and options were not covered by formal guidance at all. Instead, their accounting was based largely on analogy to existing statements and on some specific EITF issues.

The derivative debacles of 1994 provided further motivation to reform the accounting for derivatives and risk management. Hedge accounting was clearly being misused, albeit by a small minority of users of derivatives. In particular, firms were embedding speculative derivative positions in swap agreements and in structured notes. Those firms most likely would never have taken on such speculative bets if they had been required to bifurcate the positions and report the derivatives separately in their financial statements. The fiscal effect of the stand-alone derivative positions would have been much more apparent to investors. Without such disclosure, financial statements had diminished value to financial analysts and other users of these documents.

SFAS No. 133 goes a long way to remedy the inconsistency and incompleteness in existing authoritative guidance. Although many might think it does not go far enough (not all financial assets and liabilities are recorded at fair value), it does move derivative positions out of the footnotes and up onto the balance sheet itself. But a price has been paid to achieve this movement. We will illustrate in later chapters that analysts will have more difficulty interpreting certain financial information derived from statements produced under SFAS No. 133 than before.

4. The Intricacies of SFAS No. 133

Statement of Financial Accounting Standards (SFAS) No. 133, *Accounting for Derivative Instruments and Hedging Activities*, replaces portions or all of a series of prior standards, including SFAS No. 52, *Foreign Currency Translation*, SFAS No. 80, *Accounting for Futures Contracts*, and SFAS No. 119, *Disclosure about Derivative Financial Instruments and Fair Value of Financial Instruments*. Specifically, SFAS No. 133 standardizes accounting and disclosure for all derivative instruments, including the derivative portions of other contracts that have similar characteristics to the instruments covered by this rule. It introduces new accounting and disclosure procedures based on a small set of core principles.

SFAS No. 133's most far-reaching accounting change requires a firm to recognize all derivatives as assets or liabilities on the balance sheet and measure them at fair value. Prior to SFAS No. 133, most derivative instruments were recorded off balance sheet. Beginning with SFAS No. 119, they were disclosed only in the notes.

Under SFAS No. 133, gains and losses on many derivative positions, whether realized or not, are to flow into earnings in the period in which they occur. Exceptions include gains and losses on derivatives qualifying as hedges of forecasted transactions. These gains and losses are to be recorded in equity as other comprehensive income until the transactions are completed, at which time they are recycled into earnings. Thus, the accounting and disclosure differ depending on the type of hedge. If the derivative meets the criteria for a hedge, the gains and losses are matched, to the extent the hedge is effective, by the gains and losses on the item that has been hedged. Consequently, for qualifying hedges, other accounts in the balance sheet can be affected by the hedge accounting. The ineffective portion of the hedge, however, must *always* be reported in earnings in the period of mismatch.

SFAS No. 133 shifts the focus of accounting and disclosure away from individual types of instruments—for example, options, futures, forwards, and swaps—to the firm's basic objective for using the instrument. These objectives may include hedging the risk of changes in the value of an asset or liability in response to changes in an underlying variable or hedging the risk of future expected variable cash flows. The concept of hedging as risk reduction has shifted slightly to incorporate the broader notion of risk management. Although the principles seem relatively straightforward, application of the rule to specific instruments may involve considerable complexity reflecting both the inherent nature of the instruments and the continuing requirements for valuation data.

Hedge Accounting

SFAS No. 133 specifies acceptable classes of risks for hedging purposes. To qualify for hedge accounting, the identified risk to be hedged must be an acceptable risk for the class of asset or liability. For *financial* assets and liabilities, the only risks permitted to receive hedge accounting are (1) market price risk, (2) interest rate risk, (3) foreign exchange risk, and (4) credit, or default, risk. For these risks, hedge accounting specifies that gains and losses on the hedging instrument must go to earnings—or, in some cases, to other comprehensive income in equity—matched by losses and gains on the item hedged, with any hedge ineffectiveness recognized in earnings currently.

For *nonfinancial* asset and liability exposures, such as property and equipment, SFAS No. 133 permits hedge accounting for only two risks: (1) market price risk and (2) foreign exchange risk for a forecasted purchase or sale. Although managers may choose to enter into other types of hedges, these hedges will not qualify for hedge accounting treatment, which means that all gains and losses on the derivative instrument will go to earnings each period but will *not* be matched by offsetting losses and gains on the item hedged.

When a firm uses futures, forwards, swaps, or options to reduce an exposure to risk, it may be able to designate the derivative, or a portion of it, as
- a *fair-value hedge*—a hedge of the exposure to changes in the fair value of a recognized asset or liability, or of a firm commitment, that is attributable to a particular risk;
- a *cash flow hedge*—a hedge of the exposure to variability in the cash flows of a recognized asset or liability, or of a forecasted transaction, that is attributable to a particular risk; or
- a hedge of the foreign currency exposure of
  (1) a firm commitment (a *foreign currency fair-value hedge*),
  (2) an available-for-sale debt security (a *foreign currency fair-value hedge*),
  (3) a foreign-currency-denominated forecasted transaction (a *foreign currency cash flow hedge*), or
  (4) a net investment in a foreign operation.

Note that a firm commitment is an executory contract that represents both a right and an obligation.

The new standard reflects the most recent views of the Financial Accounting Standards Board (FASB) on financial disclosure (SFAS No. 133, p. 1):

- Derivatives are assets or liabilities and should be reported in the financial statements.
- Fair value is the most relevant measure for financial instruments and the only relevant measure for derivatives. Derivatives should be measured at fair value, and adjustments to the carrying amount of hedged items should reflect changes in their fair values (that is, gains and losses) that are attributable to the risk being hedged and that arise while the hedge is in effect.
- Only items that are assets or liabilities should be reported as such in the financial statements.
- Special accounting for items designated as being hedged should be provided only for qualifying transactions, and one aspect of qualification should be an assessment of offsetting changes in fair values or cash flows.

Definition of a Derivative

Among the first tasks the FASB faced as part of its effort to develop a comprehensive standard for derivative accounting, including hedge accounting, was to decide what factors distinguish a derivative from other financial instruments. The definition of a derivative instrument has been broadened under SFAS No. 133 to include many contracts that would formerly not have been considered to be derivatives. **Exhibit 4.1** summarizes the criteria for determining whether a contract is a derivative. Notice that the definition has shifted from a reliance on classic categories of derivatives to five defining characteristics. Thus, in general, a financial instrument—either the entire instrument or a portion thereof—now has to be scrutinized to determine if it meets the criteria.

The term "underlying" is a new concept in the accounting for derivatives. An underlying is *not*, per se, an asset or liability that appears on the balance sheet. An underlying in this context is a market-related characteristic of the asset or liability that gives rise to changes in value. For example, the price of a bond may vary with changes in interest rates, the creditworthiness of the issuer, or perhaps the foreign exchange (FX) rate. Any of these characteristics can be the underlying of a derivative used to manage changes in the price risk of the bond. As another example, the price of a futures contract for oil may change as the price of oil changes; the underlying is the price of oil, not the oil itself. The price, or other underlying, is thus a variable that can fluctuate with changing market circumstances.

Exhibit 4.1. Summary of Derivative and Hedging Instruments

A *derivative instrument* is a contract with the following distinguishing characteristics:

- It has one or more *underlyings*.
- It has one or more *notional amounts*.
- Its value to the holder changes by direct reference to the underlyings.
- It requires no initial net investment or an initial net investment that is smaller than would be required for other types of contracts that would be expected to have a similar response to changes in market factors.
- It can readily be settled net or its equivalent.

A *hedge*, either a derivative or the derivative portion of another contract, may be designated as one of the following:

- A *fair-value hedge* is a hedge of the exposure to changes in the fair value of a recognized asset or liability or of a *firm commitment*.
- A *cash flow hedge* is a hedge of the exposure to variability in the cash flows of a recognized asset or liability or of a *forecasted transaction*.
- A hedge of the foreign currency exposure of (1) a firm commitment or (2) an available-for-sale debt security is a *foreign currency fair-value hedge*; a hedge of the foreign currency exposure of (3) a foreign-currency-denominated forecasted transaction is a *foreign currency cash flow hedge*; or the hedge could be a hedge of the foreign currency exposure of (4) a net investment in a foreign operation.

A notional amount is a number of currency units, shares, barrels, bushels, pounds, or other units specified in the contract. The notional amount is used in conjunction with the underlying to determine the amount to be settled under the contract. The two may be simply multiplied, or a formula may be used, possibly including a leverage factor. For example, on a plain-vanilla interest rate swap, the underlying typically is LIBOR (the London Interbank Offered Rate). The dollar settlement payment is the difference between the fixed rate and LIBOR times the notional principal amount. The notional amount can be thought of as the scaling variable for determining the total amount of gain or loss.

A derivative instrument does *not* require that the holder or writer invest or receive the notional amount at the inception of the contract. The contract may require no initial investment or a small investment relative to other instruments that are sensitive to changes in the same market factors. For example, an "at-market" forward contract has an initial value of zero; no money is exchanged upon entering the transaction. An "off-market" forward contract has a forward price different from the at-market one. The party committing to the relatively unfavorable side of the off-market forward price receives an up-front payment from the counterparty that reflects the present value of the difference between the at-market price and the one on the contract. Also, an initial payment may reflect some other factor of the contract or difference in the credit ratings of the parties. The buyer of an option typically pays the premium to the writer at initiation of the contract. In each case, however, the amount of the initial payment is usually quite small in relation to the notional amount. A key provision in the definition of a derivative is that the contract must require or permit net settlement (1) in cash or in assets readily convertible to cash or (2) by a market mechanism outside the contract, for example, by taking an offsetting position to the contract on a futures exchange.

Certain securities and contracts have been specifically excluded from the definition of a derivative in SFAS No. 133. These include regular-way security trades (whereby delivery and settlement are made a few days after the trade date, according to market convention), normal inventory purchases and sales, traditional insurance contracts (i.e., life and property and casualty insurance), and most financial guarantee contracts. Traditional debt and equity securities, commercial loans, and mortgage-backed securities, which require an initial net investment of the principal amount, are not considered derivatives; however, futures and option contracts on these securities would qualify as derivatives.

Other exceptions to the definition of a derivative in the statement include over-the-counter contracts based on climatic variables, sometimes termed "weather derivatives"; options to purchase or sell real estate or machinery; contracts issued in connection with stock-based compensation arrangements; and contracts that are indexed to an entity's own stock. Some popular debt instruments that contain derivative-like features have been specifically excluded from SFAS No. 133, namely, interest-only and principal-only certificates created from the cash flows on mortgage-backed bonds. The FASB has dealt with some of these instruments separately and apparently intends to consider the remainder later in its ongoing financial instruments project.

Contracts that meet the criteria of being derivatives under SFAS No. 133 include all the familiar products—options, forwards, futures, swaps, caps, floors, collars, and warrants. In addition, many hybrid derivative instruments, for example, options on swaps (i.e., swaptions), qualify as derivatives. As a reminder, accounting and disclosure of derivative instruments no longer follow the type or name of the instrument but rather are driven by the underlying characteristics of the instrument and the objectives for which it is held, for example, hedging fair values or future cash flows. Under SFAS No. 133, managers will need to consider the terms of many types and classes of contracts commonly used in ongoing business to ascertain whether the contracts meet the definition of a derivative.

Embedded Derivatives

SFAS No. 133 requires that many (but not all) derivatives that are embedded in other contracts be bifurcated and accounted for as separate derivative instruments. Consider, for instance, a debt security issued by a commercial bank that pays interest based on the price of gold. Suppose that the interest rate is calculated each period as 2 percent plus an amount proportionate to the difference between the spot market gold price (per troy ounce) and $250. If the spot gold price is less than $250, the interest rate is just the base rate of 2 percent. This hybrid security is a straightforward note and a portfolio of option contracts on the price of gold. Under SFAS No. 133, these derivatives must be reported separately from the underlying note.

The key criterion for this bifurcation is whether the economic characteristics and risks of the embedded derivatives (the call options on gold in this example) are *clearly and closely* related to those of the host contract (the debt instrument). If so, separation is not required; if not, the derivative must be separated and accounted for as a stand-alone instrument.

Embedded derivatives are defined in SFAS No. 133 as "implicit or explicit terms that affect the cash flows or value of other exchanges required by a contract in a manner similar to a derivative." SFAS No. 133 requires that if the terms are similar in all other ways to a derivative instrument, they must be separated from the host contract and accounted for as derivatives. This provision is a major departure from traditional accounting practice. Determining if an embedded derivative must be bifurcated and treated as a derivative instrument involves answering three questions:

- Is the contract carried at fair value through earnings? (If yes, the rule does not apply.)
- Would the provision be a derivative if it were freestanding? (If no, the rule does not apply.)
- Is it clearly and closely related to the host contract? (If yes, the rule does not apply.)

Embedded derivatives not excluded by the answer to one of those questions are separated and accounted for under SFAS No. 133. Note that an affirmative response to the first question eliminates hybrid securities carried in a trading portfolio but not those that are classified as "available for sale." So, although the commercial bank issuing the notes in the previous example would pull out the embedded written call options on gold, the investment bank underwriting the notes would not do so. The investor that ultimately buys the same notes, however, might or might not have to treat the embedded options as a separable derivative under SFAS No. 133.

"Clearly and closely related" is a new qualifying expression in accounting. The expression refers to the economic characteristics of the provision and the risks involved. The factors that must be considered in deciding if the provision is an embedded derivative are (1) the type of host contract and (2) the underlying. An example of an instrument that is clearly and closely related to the host contract and thus not a separable derivative is a typical callable corporate bond. The risks and characteristics of the firm's right to buy the bond back from the investor and the host bond are deemed to be clearly and closely related. Other underlyings identified in SFAS No. 133 that would be considered to be clearly and closely related for debt hosts are interest rates (assuming they have no built-in leverage factor) and the creditworthiness of the issuer.

For example, suppose a debt instrument includes an acceleration clause advancing the maturity date should the issuer's credit rating decline (i.e., a material adverse change, or MAC, clause). This clause would be clearly and closely related to one of the basic pricing factors for such debt instruments, and thus not a separable derivative. Similarly, among the more common "preferences" used to enhance the attractiveness of preferred stock is the right to convert it to common stock, a right that could become quite valuable if the firm prospers. But because this is a traditional provision of such securities, it would not be treated as a separable derivative.

An example indicating the far-reaching changes springing from SFAS No. 133 is an equity conversion feature in a debt instrument (e.g., a typical convertible bond). The FASB reasons that the equity feature in the debt and the interest rate on the debt are *not* clearly and closely related. Therefore, the equity conversion option must be separated and treated as a derivative instrument by the investor, unless the convertible bond is held in a trading portfolio, for which all positions are already carried at fair value and gains and losses are run through the income statement. The issuer of the convertible bond, however, does *not* bifurcate the host debt and the embedded written call options on its equity price under SFAS No. 133. The standard specifically excludes "contracts that are indexed to an entity's own stock."

The structured note market that has developed in the past 15 years definitely will be affected by the embedded derivative considerations in SFAS No. 133.[1] This market caters to investors that seek to hold securities reflecting their particular views on such financial and economic variables as future interest rates, foreign exchange rates, and commodity prices. This market has been "investor-driven" in that issuers, often AAA rated federal agencies, typically transform the structured notes back into a more plain-vanilla design using derivatives provided by investment banks. Consider, again, the gold-linked notes mentioned earlier. The investor could have purchased a fixed-rate commercial bank note and a series of exchange-traded options on gold

---

[1] Crabbe and Argilagos (1994) provide a discussion of the pre-SFAS No. 133 structured note market.

prices. Some advantages may exist, however, to embedding the derivatives in the structured note—lower overall transaction costs and the availability of links to gold prices further into the future.

A fairly prosaic structure is a floating-rate note (FRN) that contains a maximum or minimum level for the variable coupon rate. Consider, for instance, a "collared FRN" that pays semiannual interest set at six-month LIBOR, subject to a maximum of 8 percent and a minimum of 4 percent. From the investor's perspective, this structured note is comparable to a straight FRN paying just LIBOR (and subject to a minimum of zero, of course) and a written interest rate cap on LIBOR at a strike rate of 8 percent and a purchased interest rate floor on LIBOR at a strike rate of 4 percent.[2]

Under SFAS No. 133, the investor might have to treat the embedded cap and floor contracts as separate derivatives, depending on the initial level of LIBOR and the strike rate. If LIBOR is between 4 percent and 8 percent, both options are out of the money. Then, the embedded derivatives do *not* have to be bifurcated. But if LIBOR is below 4 percent or above 8 percent, one of the options is in the money and must be accounted for separately. Therefore, embedded in-the-money options are subject to bifurcation but out-of-the-money options are not.

Consider a "floored FRN" on which the issuer pays LIBOR plus 0.25 percent subject to a minimum of 5 percent. Suppose that on a straight FRN (i.e., one without any embedded options) the coupon formula would have been LIBOR plus 0.40 percent. The buyer of the floored FRN presumably expects LIBOR to be below 5 percent, on average, and accepts a smaller margin over LIBOR as payment for the embedded interest rate floor. If LIBOR initially is below 5 percent, the interest rate floor is in the money and would have to be treated as a separate derivative.

An "inverse FRN" is another structured note that might or might not have to be bifurcated under SFAS No. 133. These notes have coupon interest rates that move inversely to the reference rate, for instance, 10 percent minus LIBOR. In 1994, the Orange County Investment Pool ended up with about one-fourth of its portfolio in such structures. Obviously, these notes lose value when interest rates rise. The relevant criterion in the new standard is whether the investor's rate of return could be at least double that on an otherwise

---

[2]Interest rate caps and floors are a series of over-the-counter option contracts on a reference rate, such as LIBOR. Cash settlement is made each period on a net basis as on an interest rate swap. Just as a forward contract can be decomposed into a call and a put option, an interest rate swap can be viewed as a combination of a cap and a floor—one long and the other short—at the same strike rate. An interest rate collar is a combination of a cap at a higher strike rate and a floor at a lower strike rate.

comparable note having a traditional fixed- or floating-rate coupon structure. Suppose that the issuer of the inverse floater at 10 percent minus LIBOR could issue fixed-rate debt at 5 percent for the same maturity. Then, the investor (as well as the issuer) would not have to bifurcate the embedded derivative. Suppose, however, that the structured note is a "leveraged inverse FRN" paying 15 percent minus two times LIBOR (Orange County owned some of these as well). This hybrid instrument fails the "clearly and closely related" test and would need to have its embedded derivatives separated from the host debt. If LIBOR remained below 2.5 percent, the investor's yield could be more than two times the conventional note. Observe that if LIBOR were to exceed 7.5 percent, the coupon rate would be zero.

Exactly how one is to bifurcate a structured note similar to this leveraged inverse FRN is not obvious, nor is it covered in SFAS No. 133.[3] The question is: What are the embedded derivatives in the structure? To see this problem, suppose that the going at-market swap rate is 5 percent fixed versus LIBOR. The accounting problem is that more than one combination of derivatives creates future coupon cash flows equivalent to the leveraged inverse FRN. Consider these two portfolios of notes and derivatives from the perspective of an investor:

- Buy a 5 percent fixed-rate note, enter *two* receive 5 percent fixed/pay LIBOR interest rate swaps, and buy two interest rate caps at a strike rate of 7.5 percent.
- Buy a straight FRN paying LIBOR, enter *three* receive 5 percent fixed/pay LIBOR interest rate swaps, and buy two interest rate caps at a strike rate of 7.5 percent.

These are not the only possibilities. Suppose that the issuer also can place zero-coupon notes on the market for the same maturity as the other securities. Here is another portfolio that matches the future cash flows on the leveraged inverse FRN:

- Buy a zero-coupon note, and buy *two* interest rate floors at a strike rate of 7.5 percent.

This example illustrates that the same structured note can be interpreted as three different host instruments and different packages of derivatives. **Exhibit 4.2** provides analysis of the payoffs and illustrates the equivalence of the transactions.

---

[3]This issue and a number of other issues have been under review by the FASB's Derivatives Implementation Group (DIG). Several DIG recommendations have been incorporated into SFAS No. 138, *Accounting for Certain Derivative Instruments and Certain Hedging Activities— an Amendment of FASB Statement No. 133*, issued in June 2000. SFAS No. 138 and DIG pronouncements may be obtained from the FASB Web site (www.fasb.org).

Exhibit 4.2. Rates of Return from Investor's Perspective for Various Combinations of Derivatives that Equal the Return of the Leveraged Inverse Floater

A. *Leveraged inverse floater at 15 percent − 2 × LIBOR (maximum 15 percent, minimum 0 percent).*

LIBOR	Leveraged Inverse Floater
0%	$15\% - 2 \times 0\% =$ **15%**
3	$15\% - 2 \times 3\% =$ **9**
6	$15\% - 2 \times 6\% =$ **3**
9	$15\% - 2 \times 9\% =$ **0**
12	$15\% - 2 \times 0\% =$ **0**

Note: If LIBOR > 7.5 percent, the coupon rate is zero. It does not become negative.

B. *One 5 percent fixed-rate note, two receive 5 percent/pay LIBOR swaps, two caps on LIBOR at 7.5 percent strike rate.*

LIBOR	Fixed-Rate Note	Two Swaps	Two Caps	All-In
0%	5%	$2 \times 5\% = 10\%$	$2 \times 0\% = 0\%$	**15%**
3	5	$2 \times 2\% = 4\%$	$2 \times 0\% = 0\%$	**9**
6	5	$2 \times -1\% = -2\%$	$2 \times 0\% = 0\%$	**3**
9	5	$2 \times -4\% = -8\%$	$2 \times 1.5\% = 3\%$	**0**
12	5	$2 \times -7\% = -14\%$	$2 \times 4.5\% = 9\%$	**0**

Note: When LIBOR < 7.5 percent, the caps are out of the money.

C. *One FRN at LIBOR, three receive 5 percent/pay LIBOR swaps, two caps on LIBOR at 7.5 percent strike rate.*

LIBOR	FRN at LIBOR	Three Swaps	Two Caps	All-In
0%	0%	$3 \times 5\% = 15\%$	$2 \times 0\% = 0\%$	**15%**
3	3	$3 \times 2\% = 6\%$	$2 \times 0\% = 0\%$	**9**
6	6	$3 \times -1\% = -3\%$	$2 \times 0\% = 0\%$	**3**
9	9	$3 \times -4\% = -12\%$	$2 \times 1.5\% = 3\%$	**0**
12	12	$3 \times -7\% = -21\%$	$2 \times 4.5\% = 9\%$	**0**

D. *One zero-coupon note, two floors on LIBOR at 7.5 percent strike rate.*

LIBOR	Zero-Coupon Note	Two Floors	All-In
0%	0%	$2 \times 7.5\% = 15\%$	**15%**
3	0	$2 \times 4.5\% = 9\%$	**9**
6	0	$2 \times 1.5\% = 3\%$	**3**
9	0	$2 \times 0\% = 0\%$	**0**
12	0	$2 \times 0\% = 0\%$	**0**

Note: When LIBOR > 7.5 percent, the floors are out of the money.

Structured notes that could result in a negative rate of return for the investor, even if there is no default, have to be bifurcated under SFAS No. 133. An example is a note that ties the redemption of principal to some future rate, price, or index. For instance, consider a fixed-rate note that has a formula for the redemption of principal, such as par value times the ratio of the spot price of gold to $250/ounce. If the spot price of gold is less than $250, the realized rate of return could be below zero. After this embedded long forward contract on gold prices is extracted, the remaining portions of the host must be accounted for using the generally accepted accounting principles (GAAP) that apply to the contract. The derivative must be accounted for under SFAS No. 133, including to the extent of receiving hedge treatment if it applies. Therefore, the original contract components may be dispersed in the financial statements and, quite likely, accounted for in different time periods.

Recognizing Changes in Fair Value

Under SFAS No. 133, a firm must recognize all of its derivative instruments in the balance sheet as assets or liabilities. And because derivatives must be measured at fair value, measurement of fair value should be determined in accordance with SFAS No. 107, *Disclosures about Fair Value of Financial Instruments*. Fair value is defined as "an amount at which the instrument could be exchanged in a current transaction between willing parties, other than in a forced or liquidation sale (when not readily available from a quoted market price, fair value should be estimated)." When market prices are available, the derivative is "marked to market." But when prices are not available, the derivative will have to be "marked to model." This requirement is a problem because model risk—the risk that the methodology used to estimate the value turns out to be wrong—has emerged in recent years as yet another risk to be considered in financial risk management.

The accounting for total gains and losses—that is, changes in fair value from period to period and settlement payments—depends on the reason for holding the derivative and whether it has been designated as and meets the criteria for a hedge. The following treatments of gains and losses apply, depending on the circumstances indicated:

- For a *no hedging relationship*, the gain or loss must be recognized currently in earnings.
- For a *fair-value hedge*, gains or losses on derivatives designated and qualifying as fair-value hedges must be recognized currently in earnings, together with the offsetting gain or loss on the hedged asset or liability. The effect of this treatment is that earnings are affected by any failure of the hedge instrument to track perfectly.

- For a *cash flow hedge*, the *effective* part of the gain or loss must be reported as a component of other comprehensive income (OCI)[4] outside earnings and recognized in earnings in the same period as the hedged transaction affecting earnings. The *ineffective* portion of the gain or loss on the derivative must be recognized currently in earnings. As with the fair-value hedges, any tracking error in the hedge goes to current earnings.
- For a *foreign currency hedge*, gains or losses on the instruments must be accounted for in several ways:
  - For *firm commitments*, gains and losses must be recognized currently in earnings together with the loss or gain on the hedged firm commitment.
  - For *available-for-sale securities*, gains and losses attributable to the risk being hedged must be recognized currently in earnings along with the loss or gain on the hedged security. Changes in fair value of the available-for-sale security from other nonhedged market sources would continue to go to OCI.
  - For *forecasted transactions*, the effective portion of the gain or loss on the hedging instrument of a foreign-denominated forecasted transaction must be reported as a component of OCI outside earnings and in earnings in the period that the transaction affects earnings. The ineffective portion must be recognized currently in earnings. This requirement is an expansion of prior GAAP because hedging of foreign exchange risk for forecasted transactions was generally not permitted.
  - For *hedges of the net investment in a foreign operation*, the foreign currency portion of the transaction gains and losses must be reported in OCI outside earnings. The remainder of the gain or loss must be recognized currently in earnings. This requirement is an exception to the SFAS No. 133 criterion for acceptable hedges because hedges of net positions are usually precluded under the rule.

Exhibit 4.3 summarizes the accounting for fair values and gains and losses on derivative instruments. **Exhibit 4.4** summarizes the criteria that must be met to qualify for hedge accounting.

The business press has reported widespread confusion regarding the effects on derivatives of the new reporting guidelines for gains and losses. One of the most frequently cited concerns is that SFAS No. 133 will result in increased volatility of earnings and will, therefore, discourage prudent risk

---

[4]Other comprehensive income, frequently referred to simply as comprehensive income, is a special category of unrealized earnings held as a category of shareholders' equity, but not in retained earnings, until such time as it is realized. An example is unrealized gains and losses on available-for-sale securities.

Exhibit 4.3. Summary of Income Statement and Balance Sheet Effects of Derivative and Hedging Instruments

| | Gains/Losses Recognized | | |
Derivative Instrument	Net Income	Comprehensive Income	Mark to Market in Balance Sheet
No hedging relationship	×		×
Fair-value hedge	×		×
Hedged item	×		×
Cash flow hedge			
Effective portion		×	
Ineffective portion	×		
Foreign currency hedge			
Firm commitments	×		×
Hedged firm commitment	×		×
Foreign currency portion of available-for-sale security hedge	×		×
Hedged available-for-sale security	×		×
Forecasted transaction			
Effective portion		×	
Ineffective portion	×		
Net investment in a foreign subsidiary			
Foreign currency portion of transaction gain/loss		×	
Remainder	×		×

management. In general, however, volatility will be increased *only to the extent that the hedge is ineffective.* That is, a perfect hedge will not introduce any additional volatility because all changes in the hedging instrument will be directly offset by the item being hedged. To the extent that only imperfect hedges are available, volatility can be expected to increase. On the other hand, firms will have a stronger incentive than they had before SFAS No. 133 to carefully consider the behavior of potential hedging instruments compared with that of the items they may wish to hedge.

The FASB has acknowledged the importance of selecting appropriate instruments in addressing the various types of hedges. Hedging effectiveness has not been defined in a quantitative manner in SFAS No. 133, but rather, it states that hedges should meet the qualitative criterion of being "highly effective." Because all gains and losses on hedging instruments will have to be reported currently in earnings—with the exception of the effective portion of cash flow hedges (on forecasted transactions), which will go to OCI outside earnings—this is a major reporting issue. If a hedge fails to meet the highly effective criterion, gains and losses on the derivative and the hedged item will

Exhibit 4.4. Summary of Fair Value, Cash Flow, and Foreign Currency Hedge Criteria and Provisions

Fair-Value Hedge Criteria

A hedging instrument must meet the following criteria to qualify for *fair-value* hedge accounting:

1. The hedging relationship must be formally documented.
2. The firm's risk management objective and strategy for undertaking the hedge must be presented.
3. The hedging instrument and the related item must be identified.
4. The risk being hedged must be identified.
5. The means of assessing the effectiveness of the instrument in offsetting changes in the hedged item must be specified.
6. The hedge's effectiveness must be assessed on a regular and continuing basis, when the financial statements are reported, and at least every three months.
7. It cannot be a nonderivative instrument.

Cash Flow Hedge Criteria

A hedging instrument must meet the following criteria to qualify for *cash flow* hedge accounting:

1. It must meet 1–7 under fair-value hedge criteria.
2. If used for modifying receipts or payments associated with a recognized asset or liability from one variable rate to another variable rate, the hedging instrument must link a designated asset and a designated liability, each with variable cash flows, and must be highly effective in achieving offsetting cash flows.

Additional criteria must be met for hedging anticipated transactions:

3. The hedge may be designated for either a single transaction or a pool of related transactions.
4. The hedge transaction must be expected to occur within a short period of time for the entire group.
5. All transactions in the pool must share the same risk exposure as that being hedged.
6. The transaction must be probable.
7. The uncertainty regarding the date of occurrence must be small, relative to the length of time from inception of the hedge until occurrence.
8. The transaction must be with a third party external to the entity.
9. The risk being hedged must affect reported earnings.
10. The transaction cannot be the acquisition of an asset or incurrence of a liability that following the acquisition will be remeasured with changes in fair value attributable to the hedged risk reported in earnings.
11. For held-to-maturity instruments, the risk cannot be interest rate risk.

Foreign Currency Fair-Value Hedge Criteria

A hedging instrument must meet the following criteria to qualify for *foreign currency fair-value* hedge accounting:

1. It must meet 1–6 under fair-value hedge criteria.
2. The hedge *may* be a nonderivative instrument.

Foreign Currency Cash Flow Hedge Criteria

A hedging instrument must meet the following criteria to qualify for *foreign currency cash flow* hedge accounting:

1. It must meet 1–11 under cash flow hedge criteria.
2. The entity must be a party to the transaction.
3. The transaction must be denominated in a currency other than the entity's functional currency.
4. A nonderivative financial instrument may *not* be a hedging instrument.

not receive hedge accounting treatment. That is, the derivative gain or loss in earnings will not be offset by the fair-value changes of the hedged item. No doubt, managers will want to evaluate with great care the advisability of having hedges with only limited effectiveness.

The following example illustrates the allowable methods for determining effectiveness of a hedge. A firm issues a $10,000,000, five-year, 7 percent fixed-rate note. Concurrently, the firm enters into a five-year, at-market interest rate swap with a notional principal of $10,000,000 to receive interest at a fixed rate of 6.5 percent and pay interest at a variable rate equal to LIBOR. The combination of the swap and the debt results in a net cash outflow equal to LIBOR plus 50 basis points. Both the debt liability and the swap require payments to be made or received on April 1 and October 1 of each year. As an at-market swap, no premium was paid or received upon entering the swap. The firm designates the swap as a fair-value hedge of the fixed-rate debt related to changes in the general level of market interest rates. In effect, the firm has transformed its fixed-rate debt into a synthetic floating-rate (LIBOR) obligation.[5]

The firm could assess whether the swap will be highly effective, both at the inception of the hedge and on an ongoing basis, by calculating the present value of the cash flows on the debt (principal and interest) and on the swap (estimated net cash settlements) for different interest rate scenarios and by comparing the changes in present value for those interest rate scenarios. The hedge is ineffective to the extent that those changes in present value do not offset. The present value calculations would relate only to the effect of a change in interest rates; that is, the calculations would assume fixed cash flows on the debt, regardless of a change in credit quality.

Alternatively, because the debt is fixed rate and the swap has a fixed leg and because the notional amount, payment dates, and remaining term of the swap and debt are the same in this particular circumstance, the firm does not have to perform the calculation described above. That is, because the terms are the same, the firm may assume that the hedge is highly effective. Therefore, both at inception of the hedge and on an ongoing basis, the firm can expect the hedge to be highly effective at achieving offsetting changes in fair value. This situation is known in SFAS No. 133 as the "shortcut" method for measuring effectiveness. But because SFAS No. 133 requires that hedge effectiveness be

---

[5]SFAS No. 138 redefines interest rate risk as that attributable to a *benchmark interest rate*, either the LIBOR swap rate or the rate on direct U.S. Treasury obligations. Changes in sector spreads and those attributable to a particular borrower are designated by SFAS No. 138 as *credit risk*. This provision removes a major cause of ineffectiveness for firms that chose to hedge interest rate risk alone.

reassessed at least quarterly, the quarterly reassessments will essentially require redocumenting that the shortcut criteria are still satisfied.

Fair-Value Hedge Criteria

A firm will enter into a fair-value hedge to reduce its exposure to variability in current market value resulting from a particular risk. Fair-value hedges are designated for assets, liabilities, or firm commitments that have *fixed terms*— for instance, a fixed-rate bond or a fixed price on an asset that the enterprise is firmly committed to purchase. The key point is that the value of the item will change because it has preset terms. An example of a fair-value hedge on a fixed-rate bond that has been issued is a pay floating/receive fixed interest rate swap. The derivative effectively converts the debt from fixed to floating interest payments, thereby mitigating changes in its fair value.

For a hedging instrument to qualify for fair-value hedge accounting, the firm must provide formal documentation of (1) the hedge instrument; (2) its risk management objective and strategy for undertaking the hedge, including identification of the hedging instrument and the related item; (3) the specific risk being hedged; and (4) the means of assessing the effectiveness of the instrument in offsetting changes in the hedged item.

In addition, the assessment of the hedge's effectiveness must be conducted on a regular and continuing basis, when the financial statements are reported, and at least every three months. Clearly, substantial scrutiny of both the hedging instrument and the hedged item will be required at inception of the hedge and on a continuing basis. Thus, establishing and maintaining qualifying hedges will require more resources and involve more costs than previously.

Under SFAS No. 133, gains and losses must be recognized in the current period in the income statement for both the hedging instrument and the hedged item. The balance sheet carrying amount of the hedged item must be adjusted by the change in fair value attributable to the risk hedged and to the extent hedged. The amount must be adjusted to eliminate the ineffective portion of the hedge. For hedged items reported at fair value for which gains and losses are reported in OCI—for example, an available-for-sale security— the gain or loss on the hedging instrument must be reported in earnings. This requirement could result in a mismatch of the gains and losses on the hedge and the hedged item.[6]

If the hedge criteria are no longer met for a hedging instrument or if the derivative expires or is sold, terminated, or exercised, then hedge accounting

---

[6]For foreign currency hedges, the gains and losses on both the hedge and the hedged item must be reported in current income.

must be discontinued. Moreover, when instruments are deemed to no longer meet the criterion of being highly effective, then any as yet unrecorded gains and losses on the hedged item and the hedging instrument up to that point must be recognized currently in earnings. Instruments that specifically cannot qualify as derivatives (e.g., Treasury notes) cannot be designated as hedging instruments except in the case of foreign currency hedges.

Cash Flow Hedge Criteria

A firm will use a cash flow hedge to reduce its exposure to volatility in future cash flows, for example, those arising from anticipated sales. Cash flow hedges are designated for assets, liabilities, or forecasted transactions that have *variable terms*, such as a floating-rate bond. The key point is that future cash flows will vary because the terms are not fixed.

For example, a firm may wish to enter into a pay fixed/receive floating interest rate swap to mitigate its exposure to the variability in future interest payments resulting from changes in interest rates for its floating-rate debt. The swap effectively converts the debt to a fixed-rate liability, locking in a fixed pattern of interest payments. This example can be contrasted sharply with the fair-value hedge using an interest rate swap previously discussed. That derivative in the previous example would expose the firm to potentially greater cash flow volatility by "unlocking" the fixed-coupon rate to reduce changes in fair value. Thus, depending on its risk management objectives and other balance sheet and income considerations, a firm may use interest rate swaps or other derivatives either to insulate the firm from fair-value changes in assets or liabilities, as seen in the previous section, or to reduce exposures to variability in cash flows, as in the current example. Assuming the criteria for hedges are met, both derivatives will qualify for hedge accounting, although the risk exposures and accounting will be different for the two strategies. These comparative examples clearly show that the analyst will have to consider the implications of management's hedging strategies for the firm's risk profile and exposures going forward.

Cash flow hedges have documentation and hedging effectiveness requirements and criteria at inception similar to those for fair-value hedges. Cash flow hedges may be designated for either a single transaction or a pool of related transactions, they must be expected to occur within a short period of time for the entire group, and all such transactions must share the same risk exposure as that being hedged. In addition, the transaction must be probable, and the uncertainty regarding the date of occurrence should be small, relative to the length of time from inception of the hedge until occurrence. Thus, cash flow hedges cannot be designated for anticipated transactions with a high degree of uncertainty of occurrence or uncertainty in timing. The transaction must be with a third party external to the entity, and the risk being hedged must affect reported earnings.

A particularly interesting criterion is that the transaction cannot be the acquisition of an asset (or incurrence of a liability) that subsequent to the purchase will be remeasured with changes in fair value attributable to the hedged risk reported in earnings. That is, most forecasted transactions to acquire financial instruments will be precluded.[7] For held-to-maturity instruments, the risk being hedged cannot be market interest rate risk because, by definition, market interest rate changes are not relevant for held-to-maturity instruments. The decline in creditworthiness of the issuer, however, would be a hedgable risk.

Gains and losses from the effective portion of the hedge must be reported in OCI, with the ineffective portion reported in earnings. Any part of the hedge's gain or loss that an entity's risk management strategy excludes from assessment of hedge effectiveness must be reported currently in earnings.

Those amounts that have been reported in OCI must be recycled into earnings in the same period in which the transaction occurs and is reported. If the cash flow hedge is discontinued before the date when the variability of the future cash flows associated with the hedged forecasted transaction is eliminated (because the transaction probably will not occur), all gains and losses reported in OCI must be recognized immediately in earnings.

Foreign Currency Hedges

Prior to SFAS No. 133, foreign currency hedges received specialized accounting under SFAS No. 52. Some of those provisions have been continued in SFAS No. 133. For example, an entity may designate a foreign currency hedge as (1) a fair-value hedge of a firm commitment or an available-for-sale security, (2) a cash flow hedge of a foreign-currency-denominated forecasted transaction, or (3) a hedge of a net investment in a foreign operation. Otherwise, foreign currency hedges closely follow the new accounting guidelines for other derivative securities.

All of the accounting provisions apply to foreign currency fair-value hedges of firm commitments with the exception of the prohibition against the use of nonderivative hedging instruments. That is, Treasury securities can be used. Such instruments may be used as foreign currency hedges provided

---

[7]SFAS No. 138 exempts many forward purchase and sale contracts that routinely result in physical delivery of goods or commodities but that frequently fail the "normal purchase and sale" exclusion for application of SFAS No. 133. Thus, under the new exemption, SFAS No. 133 will not have to be applied to such contracts.

that they are consistent with the entity's risk management strategy. Gains and losses from nonderivative hedges must be recognized currently in earnings. Hedges for foreign currency fair-value exposures of available-for-sale securities are to be accounted for the same as those for other fair-value hedges. Gains and losses for foreign currency fair-value hedges must also be accounted for consistently with those for other fair-value hedge instruments.

Additional criteria are required for a derivative instrument to qualify as a hedge of the variability in cash flows associated with a foreign-currency-denominated forecasted transaction, for example, a forecasted direct foreign export sale:

- The entity is a party to the transaction.
- The transaction is denominated in a currency other than the entity's functional currency.
- All other criteria are met.

A nonderivative financial instrument may *not* be designated as a hedging instrument in a foreign currency cash flow hedge. The accounting is otherwise identical to that of other cash flow hedges.

Foreign currency transaction gains or losses on hedges of the foreign currency exposure of a net investment in a foreign operation must be reported in the same manner as the translation adjustment if the hedge is designated as and is effective as an economic hedge of the exposure. Any difference between the hedging gain or loss and the translation adjustment must be reported in earnings.

SFAS No. 133 Disclosures

SFAS No. 133 mandates that firms that use derivatives make certain qualitative and quantitative disclosures. The disclosures include

- the firm's objectives for holding the derivatives;
- the context needed to understand the objectives and strategies for achieving the objectives;
- separate categories of description for fair-value hedging instruments, cash flow hedges, foreign currency exposure hedges, and all other derivatives; and
- the risk management policy for each type of hedge, including a description of the items or transactions for which risks are hedged.

Specific derivative types have their own set of disclosure requirements. These include

- for derivatives not designated as hedges, the purpose of the derivative activity;

- for fair-value hedges, the net gain or loss of the ineffective portion of the hedge that is recognized in earnings and any gain or loss excluded from the assessment of the hedge effectiveness and the amount of gains and losses recognized in earnings when a hedged firm commitment no longer qualifies as a fair-value hedge;
- for cash flow hedges, the same items as for fair-value hedges but also a description of the transactions or other events that will result in the recognition in earnings of gains and losses that are deferred in OCI, the amount of deferred gains and losses that will be recognized in the next 12 months, and the amount of gains and losses recognized in earnings as a result of the discontinuance of cash flow hedges (because the original forecasted transaction probably will not occur);
- for hedges of the net investment in a foreign operation, the net amount of gains or losses included in cumulative translation adjustments; and
- for nonhedging derivatives, the separate amounts of gains and losses on the derivatives disaggregated by business activity, risk, or other category that is consistent with the management of that activity.

In the transition from off-balance-sheet disclosure in SFAS No. 119 to on-balance-sheet fair market values with most gains and losses reported in current income, the FASB decided to relax a number of the specific disclosures required in SFAS No. 119. Among the disclosures useful to analysts that are no longer required are (1) the separate amounts of derivative gains and losses and indicators of the effects of derivative use on earnings and (2) the notional principal of derivatives by category of instruments, which was frequently used as an indicator of the relative intensity of use of derivatives.

The FASB contemplated the requirement that a firm disclose the line items in the income statement where derivative gains and losses are included but did not require the information in the final statement.[8] Thus, derivative gains and losses, although largely accounted for in earnings, will be, for the most part, invisible. Moreover, to the extent that a firm successfully argues that hedge ineffectiveness components are not material, this information similarly will be invisible.

SEC Derivative Disclosure Requirements

The U.S. Securities and Exchange Commission (SEC) has expanded the disclosure requirements for "market risk sensitive instruments" in Release No. 33-7386 and also in amendments to other rules. The new rule expands

---

[8]This information is required for hedge ineffectiveness amounts or amounts excluded from the hedge effectiveness assessment.

existing disclosure regarding accounting policies for derivatives as well as required quantitative and qualitative information about market risk inherent in risk-sensitive instruments. These new disclosures should be outside the financial statements and notes and will likely be included in other SEC-required disclosures, such as the management discussion and analysis of operations and financial condition. These disclosures are significant because they provide information important to analysts that is not inherently included in the SFAS No. 133 disclosures. Recall that the primary focus of SFAS No. 133 is on fair-value recording of derivatives in the balance sheet with gains and losses recorded in earnings each period. The SEC disclosures, which are focused on risk exposures, are more forward looking. Release No. 33-7386 specifically mentions the 1994 derivative losses experienced by some entities as motivation for the current rule.

Qualitative disclosures required by the SEC include the following:

- a registrant's primary market risk exposures at the end of the current reporting period;
- how the registrant manages those exposures; and
- changes in either the registrant's primary market risk exposures or how those exposures are managed as compared with the most recent reporting period and what is known or expected in future periods.

Quantitative disclosures may be made using one or more of the following:

- tabular presentation of fair-value information and contract terms relevant to determining future cash flows, categorized by expected maturity dates;
- sensitivity analysis expressing the potential loss in future earnings, fair values, or cash flows from selected hypothetical changes in market rates and prices; or
- value-at-risk disclosures expressing the potential loss in future earnings, fair values, or cash flows from market movements over a selected period of time and with a selected likelihood of occurrence.

Clearly, these disclosure requirements currently permit managers wide latitude in deciding how much and what type of information to disclose. Evidence from 10-K disclosures indicates that firms have responded to these requirements in a wide variety of ways, in some cases all but challenging the force of the requirements by reporting very little information, even though they use derivatives extensively. Nonetheless, these disclosures of risk exposures should be reviewed seriously by analysts.

Summary

By bringing derivative instruments, previously off balance sheet, onto the balance sheet with most gains and losses reported currently in earnings, SFAS

No. 133 has gone a long way toward correcting a major deficiency in financial reporting. This change has made a clear improvement in the quality of earnings reported to investors, creditors, and other users of financial statements. At the same time, by reducing substantially the amount of detailed disclosure in the notes regarding derivatives and their use, associated gains and losses, notional principals, and the like available under the now-superseded SFAS No. 119, much of the information formerly available to statement users for assessing *potential risk exposures* to the firm has been lost.

5. Accounting and Financial Statement Analysis for Derivative and Hedging Instruments under SFAS No. 133

The previous chapters have described the requirements for balance sheet and income statement disclosure of a firm's derivative use and risk exposures. Analysts, investors, creditors, and other users of financial statements must be able to understand and evaluate a firm's objectives in using derivative instruments and the effects of risk management strategies on corporate operations and financial performance.

Generally, one of an analyst's research objectives is to gain insight into the effects of a firm's derivative policies and usage on its potential risk exposures and profitability. As Chapter 2 discusses, firms, especially large ones, use derivatives to manage risk exposures and enhance long-run profitability. For example, firms engaged in the production and sale of commodities, or that require commodities as inputs, routinely use futures contracts to hedge against future adverse price changes. Other firms use swaps to manage interest rate risk or to provide a cash inflow and outflow pattern more consistent with operations. And still other firms use forward contracts to manage foreign exchange risk exposures. Recent history, however, has shown that financial, as well as nonfinancial firms, sometimes use derivatives to act on a market view or to otherwise speculate on future market behavior, and these speculative strategies can lead to sudden, large losses.

This chapter offers a series of examples that explain and illustrate Statement of Financial Accounting Standards (SFAS) No. 133, *Accounting for Derivative Instruments and Hedging Activities*, disclosures for derivatives and the use of these disclosures in financial analysis. Specifically, the examples address the following typical analyst questions:

- What is management required to disclose (and where) regarding its policies and objectives for using derivatives?

- How are derivatives disclosed in the balance sheet, income statement, statement of shareholders' equity (including comprehensive income), and the notes?
- How extensively does the firm use derivatives?
- What information is available regarding the timing and the magnitude of the effects of the instruments on fair market values in the balance sheet and gains and losses in the income statement?
- How has the ineffectiveness of derivatives used as hedges affected the level and volatility of income and the value of shareholders' equity?
- What portion of gains and losses reported in the balance sheet and income statement is unrealized?

In addition, examples of a large firm's (Time Warner's) disclosures under the new rules are provided and incorporated into the analysis. As firms develop experience with the disclosures, they may deviate somewhat from the presentations provided here. Moreover, firms' policies and their usage of individual instruments will differ according to the nature of their business, size, risk exposures, tradition, and the like. But because SFAS No. 133 has shifted the disclosure focus away from types of instruments to classes of risks and strategies for managing those risks, the required disclosures have coalesced. Thus, despite differences between firms in the specific instrument used to hedge—for example, a given interest rate risk exposure—the income statement, balance sheet, and shareholders' equity will capture the economic effects on each firm from the hedge, with discussion in the notes highlighting the types of instruments and strategy. SFAS No. 133 is detailed and explicit in the disclosures required so that similar information can be expected to be available for all reporting firms at some future date.

Disclosure Policies and Strategies

SFAS No. 133 requires that a firm provide certain disclosures regarding its use of derivatives. These include

- the objectives for holding or issuing those instruments,
- the context needed to understand those objectives, and
- the strategies for achieving the objectives.

The description provided must distinguish between

- derivatives designated as fair-value hedging instruments,
- derivatives designated as cash flow hedging instruments,
- derivatives used as hedges of the foreign currency exposure of a net investment in a foreign operation, and
- all other derivatives.

In addition, the discussion must include the firm's risk management policy for each of the classes of hedges as well as for the items or transactions for which risks are hedged. Discussion must include policies for derivatives that are not designated as hedging instruments.

In theory, SFAS No. 133 disclosures should be transparent, thorough, and useful in clarifying the reasons management has chosen to use derivatives and the likely extent of the effects of the derivatives on the balance sheet, income statement, and risk exposures. SFAS No. 133 provides for a minimal level of required disclosure of policies and strategies, but firms may, at their discretion, provide more information that they deem to be useful in managing market perceptions of their operations while minimizing liability exposure arising from the disclosures themselves. That is, managers must weigh the gains to be realized from providing additional exposure against the risks inherent in providing too much detail to investors and competitors. No doubt, some firms will see the disclosures as an opportunity to gain competitive advantage by conveying information to investors and creditors about their relatively low-risk profiles and the tightness and conservatism of their risk management policies and practices. These firms can be expected to voluntarily provide lengthy descriptions in the notes, possibly even providing tables that detail by class or use the notional amounts, fair market values, gains and losses, where the items appear in the statements, and the like.

In practice, however, other firms may treat the *required* minimum qualitative disclosures as the maximum necessary and provide generic boilerplate policy "discussions" that need change little, if at all, from year to year and that will be as vague as the rules permit. That is, a firm may provide sufficient discussion to meet minimal SFAS No. 133 requirements while providing little, if any, enlightenment to users of the statements. Thus, the first task of the analyst is to determine how forthcoming management has been in providing disclosures and the implications of the firm's likely risk position relative to other firms. In addition, an analyst may seek more detailed information from management to better understand the firm's policies and risk positions.

The following sections illustrate, using a series of hypothetical examples, how a firm would account for an open or nonhedging position in derivatives, derivatives used as fair-value hedges (with a reported example), cash flow hedges, and foreign currency derivatives and hedges. The disclosures under SFAS No. 133 for a public firm are provided in the relevant sections.

Derivatives Not Qualifying as Hedging Instruments

This section describes, and provides an example of, the accounting and financial statement analysis for a firm using derivatives that do not qualify as hedging instruments. For some of the following examples, we will assume a hypothetical firm, Transcontinental Agricultural Products (TAP), an internationally diversified producer, processor, and shipper of agricultural products.

Example 1: Derivative Used in an Unhedged Position. This example considers a relatively simple and straightforward situation: a derivative that either does not qualify for hedge accounting or was intended as a speculative position.

■ *Background.* In 2000, TAP buys a number of option contracts for the purchase of several currencies. The contracts expire at various dates in early 2001. The total of the premiums for the options, which were paid at inception of the contract, is $222,500. These contracts are not designated as hedges because they do not meet all of the criteria for hedge accounting, although TAP's managers believe that some possible risk exposures may be partially offset by potential gains on the contracts and they desire to purchase some insurance against losses. For simplicity, we will assume that the options expire unexercised in 2001.

■ *Disclosure and financial analysis.* At year-end 2000, TAP prepares its financial statements for the fourth quarter and the annual report. The fair market value of the contracts, including intrinsic value, is $50,000. Although the contracts have not been exercised, the loss on the options—$172,500 ($222,500 – $50,000)—cannot be deferred and must be reported as an expense currently in the income statement, even though the contracts do not expire until 2001.

The losses may be classified in any of several expense line items—for example, cost of goods and services sold, selling, general and administrative expense, or other income and expense—according to TAP's purpose in purchasing them. The gain, or in this case loss (net of tax effect), must be included in earnings in the income statement and in retained earnings in the balance sheet. SFAS No. 133 does not require disclosure of the location of the derivative gains and losses in the income statement. So, unless the firm chooses to voluntarily disclose this information, it will not be available to the analyst. The effects of the option contracts on TAP's income statement and balance sheet, ignoring tax effects and other items, are similar to those shown in **Exhibit 5.1a**. The fair market value (FMV)—$50,000—becomes the new valuation basis for recognition of gains and losses in the next period. If, instead, of declining in value, the options had a year-end fair value of $400,000, the statements would be similar to those in **Exhibit 5.1b**. Any gain or loss on the contracts in the following year—that is, beyond those gains and losses already

Exhibit 5.1a. Statement Effects of Derivatives (Option Contracts) Used in Nonhedged Positions Immediately after Purchase

Assets =		Liabilities +	Equity	
Cash	($222,500)		Retained earnings	($172,500)
Option contracts at FMV	50,000			
Total	($172,500)		Total	($172,500)
			Income Statement	
			Revenues	
			Expenses	
			Loss on purchased options	($172,500)
			Other	
			Net Income	($172,500)

Note: In order to focus solely on derivative instrument effects, this example ignores effects of other transactions on the statements. Balance sheet at December 31, 2000.

Exhibit 5.1b. Statement Effects of Derivatives (Option Contracts) Used in Nonhedged Positions Immediately prior to Sale

Assets =		Liabilities +	Equity	
Cash	($222,500)		Retained earnings	$177,500
Option contracts at FMV	400,000			
Total	$177,500		Total	$177,500
			Income Statement	
			Revenues	
			Expenses	
			Other	
			Net gain on option contracts	$177,500
			Net Income	$177,500

Note: In order to focus solely on derivative instrument effects, this example ignores effects of other transactions on the statements. Balance sheet at December 31, 2000.

recognized in 2000—would be recognized in 2001. This simple example illustrates the full implications of fair-value-model accounting with gains and losses recorded in income:

- Assets are recorded at fair market value at the end of the reporting period, or daily for most financial institutions.
- All future changes in fair value must be recognized in the periods in which they occur.

- Associated gains and losses must be fully recognized in earnings as they accrue, rather than being deferred.
- Balance sheets and income statements must reflect all fair values and associated changes *whether realized or not.*

The fair-value model is a marked contrast to the largely cash-basis model (summarized below) for derivatives that was the general rule prior to SFAS No. 133:

- Gains and losses on derivative instruments were recognized in earnings only when realized, either when margin was posted on exchange-traded contracts or when the contracts closed for over-the-counter (OTC) instruments.
- Fair value was recognized in the balance sheet only to the extent that gains and losses had been recognized in earnings.

▧ *Financial statement analysis implications summary.* The following summarizes the analysis and implications for derivatives not qualifying as hedging instruments:

- All derivative instruments must be shown at fair market value in the balance sheet (either $50,000 or $400,000 in this example).
- No shelter or deferral exists for a derivative that is not intended to, or cannot, qualify for hedge accounting. Because no offsetting hedged item position in another asset or liability exists, any associated gains or losses must be recognized in income *as they accrue*, regardless of the expiration date of the derivative.
- The SFAS No. 133 fair market value model *generally* provides for recognition of all gains and losses that have occurred to date, whether realized in cash or not. (Exceptions will be covered in later examples.) This model is a major departure from the interim SFAS No. 119 that generally has allowed accrued gains and losses that had not yet resulted in cash inflows or outflows to be deferred off the balance sheet. The result was that only those exchange-traded derivatives for which either premiums were paid or margin had to be posted were marked to market with gains and losses recognized currently. Forward contracts and interest rate swaps, the largest segment of the derivative market at present, were usually not marked to market and gains and losses were deferred. The potential for large losses to accrue off balance sheet was high, as was shown for Gibson Greetings in Chapter 3. *Now, even for contracts that over the long term are expected to result in large gains, managers will have to consider their willingness to accept, disclose, and absorb in income large short-term losses if the derivatives are used for nonhedging purposes.*

- Observe that, because all gains and losses must be recognized as they accrue, *firms that continue to use unhedged positions in derivatives are likely to experience greater volatility in income than previously* because earnings will be directly affected by the exposure to market risks, such as price and interest rate changes. This result may have the indirect effect of shifting firms to more-conservative risk and risk management positions but may not necessarily reduce managers' use of derivatives.

Fair-Value Hedges

Conceptually, accounting for fair-value hedges under SFAS No. 133 is relatively straightforward:

- The derivative is disclosed at fair market value in the balance sheet.
- The portion of the change in the fair value of the hedged asset, liability, or firm commitment *attributable to the risk being hedged* is recognized in the balance sheet to the extent that exposure has been hedged.
- All fair-value gains and losses recognized in the balance sheet, including any portion of the change in fair value of the derivative resulting from ineffectiveness, must be recognized currently in earnings.

Several implications arise from this disclosure. First, not all of the changes in fair value of the item hedged must be recognized currently. Changes in the fair value of an asset or liability may occur for a number of reasons, but only those changes directly attributable to the risk being hedged must be recognized currently. For example, the fair value of a fixed-income bond will change because of changes in market interest rates or the credit rating of the issuer. If the derivative is stated to be a hedge of interest rates, any change in bond value associated with its credit rating will not be reflected in the carrying value on the balance sheet. Second, fair-value changes must be recognized only to the extent that the firm has entered into hedges for the item. For example, the firm could decide to hedge only 50 percent of the exposure, a relatively common practice. In this case, only half of the total change arising from the hedged risk exposure would be recognized. Third, no gains and losses of a derivative contract used as a fair-value hedge can be deferred but must flow to income currently, including any gains or losses resulting from ineffectiveness. For example, should the derivative contract represent 150 percent of the amount of the item being hedged, then all of the derivative gains and losses must still be recognized currently. These implications are important for financial analysis, and we will examine them more closely.

Fair-value hedges are derivatives used to hedge the exposure to changes in fair value of a recognized asset or liability, or a firm commitment, resulting from changes in a source of market risk. When a firm holds assets or liabilities or has entered into contracts with *fixed terms*, it is exposed to the risk of loss in value as market conditions and prices change. Because a fair-value hedge effectively releases or "unlocks" fixed contractual terms, allowing the terms of the hedged item to float with market changes, the exposure to *fair-value* gains and losses is removed. A consequence of the release or unlocking of fixed terms, however, is that the firm is then "exposed" to the full range of possible outcomes, both favorable and negative.

The definition of "hedging" has shifted in SFAS No. 133 from actions taken to reduce risk to "management of risk." Such management of risk may have the effect of increasing a firm's exposure to risk. For example, a receive fixed/pay floating interest rate swap could be used to effectively convert fixed-rate debt to floating. Thus, the firm will benefit if interest rates decline. On the other hand, increases in interest rates will expose the firm to higher interest costs than it would have had under the fixed terms. In Chapter 3, we showed that Gibson Greetings used such a strategy in 1994 with a leveraged swap and incurred large losses when interest rates rose sharply in a short period of time. In the past, derivative instruments were commonly used by firms to act on a "view" regarding future movements in market prices, interest rates, and the like. Under SFAS No. 133, which generally recognizes gains and losses on derivatives as they occur, accounting means that accounting managers will be compelled to face up immediately to the consequences of any such actions: Gains and losses can no longer be deferred off the balance sheet and outside earnings.

Given the choice, firms prefer to treat a derivative instrument used as a hedge as a fair-value hedge rather than a cash flow hedge because the effect of the fair-value hedge on the income statement is relatively benign. To the extent that the hedge is highly effective, gains and losses on the derivative and the item hedged will directly offset one another, minimizing the effect on income and avoiding the introduction of additional volatility to income. If the hedge is perfect—that is, if fair-value changes offset 100 percent—income will not be affected. Because income flows directly to equity, the same is true for equity.

Accounting for fair-value hedges requires that any gains and losses accruing to the derivative used as a fair-value hedge *and* to the item hedged (to the extent the derivative is designated as a hedge of the item) be recognized currently in income. As discussed previously, this treatment may lead to partial recognition of gains and losses on the hedged item. Thus, SFAS No. 133 may lead to *partial* fair-value accounting for hedged balance sheet items or firm commitments. In addition, *any gains or losses occurring prior to the inception of the fair-value hedge are not recognized in fair-value hedge accounting.* Put differently, the inception of the fair-value hedge does not trigger full fair-value accounting on a historical basis for the item hedged. Only those fair-value changes occurring after the inception of the hedge that are attributable to the risk being hedged will produce fair-value accounting in the balance sheet with gain and loss recognition in the income statement. Thus, although SFAS No. 133 calls for fair-value recording for hedged assets and liabilities, the resulting values will not be equivalent to fair market values. The rule will typically produce only a partial mark-to-market accounting for the items for the period since the hedge was initiated.

The partial mark-to-market impact of SFAS No. 133 inherently requires that the effects of the various risk factors influencing a hedged item be identifiable, separable, and measurable. For example, for a hedged fixed-debt obligation, the firm must be able to separately measure fair-value changes in the obligation resulting from changes in market interest rates (including shifts in and movement over time along the yield curve), credit changes, the value of any call options, and other factors. SFAS No. 133 has brought a dramatic change both in the amount of accounting measurement required and in the precision of the measures. These requirements may be contrasted with those of traditional cost-based accounting that stipulate that the firm must record assets and liabilities at invoice price or fair market value on date of acquisition or issue without further market measurement requirements of any sort during the life of the item. Two exceptions to the latter include usual receivables and inventory accounting with required adjustments of the balances to estimated net realizable values. These adjustments, however, do not require partitioning of adjustments by source of risk (e.g., economic recession, decline in credit-worthiness of the customer, change in market prices, etc.).

For the case in which a hedge is perfectly effective in offsetting changes in the fair value of the asset or liability hedged, the application of SFAS No. 133 has the *effect* of deferring gains and losses on the derivative just as would have occurred prior to SFAS No. 133. The deferral may continue so long as the hedge is in effect. The Financial Accounting Standards Board (FASB) has indicated that this result was its intent. But it immediately opens a door to possible interperiod manipulation of earnings by shifting gain or loss recognition from one period to another. Recall that fair-value hedges may be used for only those assets and liabilities that under normal accounting practice would not be marked to market in the balance sheet. Use of a derivative as a fair-value hedge will effectively accelerate the recognition of any gain or loss for the risk hedged accruing currently to the item. The cost basis will be adjusted for the gain or loss in the balance sheet. That is, an asset that minus the hedge would have remained at cost will now be marked to fair value to the extent its risk has been hedged. Later, if such a formerly hedged item, such as an asset, is sold, the effect of the hedge on fair-value recognition will reverse in recognition of the gain or loss on disposal.

For example, assume that during Year 1, a firm holding an asset at its historical cost of $800 decides to enter into a derivative contract that is perfectly effective in hedging changes in the value of the asset caused by a particular risk. Also, assume that the asset increases in value by $200 over the hedging period as a result of the risk. During the hedging period, the asset is adjusted for the new fair-value increments in the balance sheet, $200, while the increases are completely offset in earnings by the negative fair-value changes in the derivative, $200, thus resulting in no net effect on earnings. No requirement exists, however, that the gain on the asset be matched on the same income statement line item as the loss on the derivative. Thus, the firm could choose, for example, to treat the gain on the asset as "operating income" and the derivative loss as "nonoperating," and the firm would not be required to disclose the location of the two components. At the end of the hedging period, the end of Year 1, the new partial fair-value basis of the asset is $1,000 ($800 cost plus the gain of $200). Furthermore, assume that the asset is sold early in Year 2 for $1,050. A gain of $50 must be shown in Year 2's income— $1,050 less the previously recognized cost plus recognized gain (i.e., $1,050 minus $1,000). The net effect of this treatment is to partially accelerate gain recognition on the asset and alter the operating results that would have otherwise been reported for both Year 1 and Year 2. That is, absent the hedge, the full gain of $250 ($1,050 less the cost of $800) would have been recognized in Year 2. In the same manner, losses also can be deferred.

The foregoing discussion clearly shows that accounting for fair-value hedges under SFAS No. 133 departs from traditional accounting practice in another profound way: *For the fair-value hedged portion of balance sheet items, SFAS No. 133 accounting provisions override other accounting principles for the item that may otherwise apply.* This result is a remarkable departure for a U.S. generally accepted accounting principles (GAAP) rule because it grants super-rule status to SFAS No. 133. Its position, however, is entirely consistent with the nature of derivative instruments used as fair-value hedges. By their very nature, they transform in some way one or more of the fixed characteristics of the item hedged. For example, many assets are currently accounted for at amortized historical cost. Assume that a firm chooses to hedge a portion of the fair value of such an asset with a derivative instrument. Then, SFAS No. 133 causes the hedged portion of the asset to be marked to fair value each period with the resulting gain or loss flowing to income at the same time, along with the fair-value change in the derivative. In addition to overriding other accounting rules, any ineffectiveness in the hedging relationship must also be recorded in income as it arises. Several closely related rules will not be suspended by SFAS No. 133 during the term of the hedge, including lower-of-cost-or-market rules for inventory and recognition of impairment of long-lived assets under SFAS No. 121, *Accounting for the Impairment of Long-Lived Assets and for Long-Lived Assets to Be Disposed Of.* That is, although partial fair-value recognition will occur with SFAS No. 133, a long-lived asset must still be reviewed for impairment in value.

Once the hedging relationship has ended, accounting for the hedged asset or liability reverts to prehedge accounting practice for that asset but at the posthedge basis. For example, assets would be subject to the usual amortization requirements and impairment of value tests. If the fair-value hedge is for a financial instrument with fixed interest, the fair-value adjustments must be recorded and amortized as adjustments to the yield to maturity on the instrument, which is consistent with the stated objective for entering into the fair-value hedge.

Example 2: Derivative Used as a Fair-Value Hedge of a Commodity Inventory. This example considers accounting and disclosure for some derivative transactions that have been used widely for a long time—commodity forward contracts. It clearly illustrates some of the most far-reaching effects of SFAS No. 133.

■ *Background.* TAP is a major producer of commodity agricultural products and uses derivatives extensively to hedge changes in the fair value of inventories. Early in 2000, TAP enters into an arrangement to hedge one type of grain inventory that cost $15,000,000 to produce (i.e., to grow, harvest, and process for storage) by selling forward contracts. The fair market value of the inventory is $18,000,000 on the contract trade date. The contracts extend beyond the current fiscal year and are for the exact same commodity as the inventory and delivered to the same geographical location. The notional principal of the forward contracts and the *fair market value* (which differs from cost by the profit margin) of the inventory hedged are the same ($18,000,000), and no premium is paid or received. The derivative qualifies for and is designated as a fair-value hedge of the inventory, and the firm intends that the derivative will hedge the entire gain or loss of the inventory. On the last day of 2000, the fiscal year-end, the derivative contracts have a fair value of $565,000 and the inventory has declined in fair value by $565,000. Management decides to sell the inventory and close out the derivative contracts on that date.

■ *Disclosure and financial analysis.* The underlying in this example is the market price of the inventory. The selling price of the inventory is $17,435,000 (the $18,000,000 initial fair market value minus the decline in value, $565,000). The cash received from closing out the derivative contract, however, is

$565,000. Thus, the gain on the contract has exactly offset the loss in fair value of the inventory. Had TAP sold the inventory on the inception date of the derivative contract, the gross profit would have been $3,000,000 ($18,000,000 – $15,000,000). The gross profit on the date it was finally sold and the forward contract was settled is also $3,000,000 ($17,435,000 – $15,000,000 + $565,000).

Firms involved in the production and sale of many commodities are permitted to recognize profits on the commodity inventories when production is completed, rather than having to wait for transfer of the inventory to the purchaser as in other industries. This mark-to-market accounting practice derives specifically from the existence of derivative markets that support such commodity producers by providing a mechanism for the immediate forward sale under contract of the inventories. Typically, futures contracts are used for agricultural products. But accounting for the contract would be greatly complicated by posting of margin over the contract period and recognition of daily mark-to-market charges. Thus, a simpler forward contract has been assumed. Aside from the cash flow effects, the net effect under SFAS No. 133 on the balance sheet and income statement is the same for both types of derivatives.

Just before the sale of the inventory on December 31, 2000, the effects on TAP's balance sheet and income statement, ignoring tax effects and other items, would be as shown in **Exhibit 5.2a**. Immediately after the sale of the inventory, and closing out and settlement of the forward contracts (ignoring tax effects and other items), the effects on TAP's balance sheet and income statement would be similar to **Exhibit 5.2b**.

▨ *Financial statement analysis implications.* The following summarizes the analysis and implications for a derivative used as a fair-value hedge of a commodity inventory:
- Effectively, by entering into the derivative contract, TAP hedged the gross profit that could have been realized early in 2000 had the inventory been directly sold, eliminating the possibility of further loss but at a cost of further gain. This result is, of course, heavily dependent on the availability of a perfect (effectively) costless hedge—a result of identical notional principal amounts and precisely the same underlyings. So long as such a hedge is available, the net result will be the same even if the gains and losses are much larger or smaller because they will offset exactly. Had such a perfect hedge not been available, a hedge using a near commodity could have been used in a so-called cross-hedge if the hedge was deemed to be highly effective in offsetting fair-value changes in the inventory. The gain on the cross-hedge derivative, however, may have been greater or less than the decline in the fair value of the inventory.

Exhibit 5.2a. Statement Effects of Derivatives (Forward Contracts) Used to Hedge the Fair Market Value of a Commodity Inventory (No Ineffectiveness)

Assets =		Liabilities +	Equity	
Inventory	$18,000,000		Retained earnings	$ 3,000,000
Allowance to reduce value of inventory to market	(565,000)		Total	$ 3,000,000
Net inventory stated at realizable value	$17,435,000			
FMV of forward contract	565,000			
Total	$18,000,000			

	Income Statement
Revenues	
Sales	$17,435,000
Expenses	
Cost of goods sold	(15,000,000)
Gross Profit	$ 2,435,000
Other	
Gain on forward contract	565,000
Net Income	$ 3,000,000

Note: In order to focus solely on derivative instrument effects, this example ignores effects of other transactions on the statements. Balance sheet at December 31, 2000.

- Regardless of whether TAP had actually chosen to sell the inventory and close out the derivative contract at year-end, the effects on the income statement would be the same: The loss on the inventory for 2000 exactly matched the gain on the derivative. This result is one of the most far-reaching effects of SFAS No. 133 and is consistent with the trend toward mark-to-market accounting.

- Exchange-traded derivative contracts generally require daily posting of margin. Consequently, prior to SFAS No. 133, in order to account for the cash payments, the fair market values of the contracts were recognized in the balance sheet with gains and losses recorded in earnings as they were realized. Similarly, commodity inventories hedged by the contracts would have been marked to market, as indicated in Example 1 and 2. But had the contracts not been exchange traded—that is, if some form of OTC forward contract were used—the gains and losses would have been deferred off the balance sheet and no recognition in earnings would have occurred until the contracts were closed and the inventory was sold. As

Exhibit 5.2b. Statement Effects of Derivatives (Forward Contracts) Used to Hedge the Fair Market Value of a Commodity Inventory Immediately after Sale (No Ineffectiveness)

Assets =		Liabilities +	Equity	
Cash	$3,000,000		Retained earnings	$ 3,000,000
Total	$3,000,000		Total	$ 3,000,000
			Income Statement	
			Revenues	
			Sales	$17,435,000
			Expenses	
			Cost of goods sold	(15,000,000)
			Gross Profit	2,435,000
			Other	
			Gain on forward contract	565,000
			Net Income	$ 3,000,000

Note: In order to focus solely on derivative instrument effects, this example ignores effects of other transactions on the statements. Balance sheet at December 31, 2000.

Chapter 2 makes clear, however, the usual practice for these commodities is to use futures contracts, as indicated in this example. Now, with fair-value accounting, the two will generally be reflected in the balance sheet and income statement the same way, with the exception of the margin cash flows on the exchange-traded contracts.

- In the example, the gain on the futures contract was shown as other income in the income statement for simplicity. In theory, however, the gain could be handled in several ways. The gain could be offset against the inventory fair-value loss in the revenues section of the income statement. This latter treatment would most closely reflect the economic motivation underlying the hedge: to preserve the gross margin that would have been realized had the inventory been sold on the date the hedge was entered. Firms may well have an incentive to choose this disclosure because it would not only enhance the revenues line item, to the extent that the hedge is effective in offsetting losses, but would, for the same reason, also have a positive effect on revenue growth rates as well as ratios that incorporate revenues. A firm that chooses to treat the gain similarly to the example will show a lower gross profit and a gain separately elsewhere, for instance, in other income. Thus, the effects are dispersed in the income statement, but income is the same regardless.

Under SFAS No. 133, the firm is not required to disclose the location of the derivative gain in the income statement or what the effect of the treatment is on gross margins. As a result, the potential exists for considerable manipulation of disclosures *within* the income statement, which is not a new problem to accounting. For example, firms have shown a tendency to move favorable outcomes higher in the income statement and to aggregate negative ones much lower, below conventional operating earnings measures. To the extent a firm uses derivatives, yet another opportunity may exist for manipulation.

- A direct implication of the lack of required disclosure regarding the location of the derivative gains and losses in the income statement is that it will be impossible for an analyst to disentangle the relative effects of derivative and nonderivative activities on the various line items in the income statement unless management chooses to voluntarily disclose the necessary information.

- Clearly, the individual line items in the balance sheet will be affected differently depending on whether the inventory remains or is sold and whether the derivative is in place or closed out.

- Before SFAS No. 133, accounting for derivatives tended to follow the recording of cash flows. That is, changes in the value of derivatives generally were recorded in the income statement and balance sheet only when received or paid in cash. As a consequence, only exchange-traded derivatives, futures, and options were marked to market before maturity and settlement of the instrument. OTC instruments—including forwards and the largest category of derivatives in use, swaps—were off balance sheet, and gains and losses were recorded in income only if paid or received in cash. SFAS No. 133 has standardized the accounting for all instruments, regardless of whether they are exchange traded or not and irrespective of the timing of cash flows. *Thus, balance sheet and income statement recognition of gains and losses will no longer coincide with cash flow statement recognition. Because the gains and losses are accrued in income, the noncash portions will have to be adjusted for in the calculation of operating cash flows. The analyst should be alert to the effects of large noncash accruals for derivatives when assessing the quality of earnings.*

Example 3. Derivative Used as a Partially Ineffective Fair-Value Hedge of a Commodity Inventory. In Example 2, the outcome of the derivative-hedging transaction and the effects on the financial statements were heavily dependent on the fact that a perfect hedge was available, thus resulting in no net gain or loss from changing market prices to TAP. This result is possible in some cases, particularly in the commodity and currency markets, where both the notional principal and the underlyings are exactly the same. This situation occurs most commonly when derivative markets have developed products especially to support particular industries by bridging market imperfections—for example, differences in the timing of commodity production and eventual sale, as in the example above, or when an established demand for currencies exists. Increasingly, however, firms desire to hedge at least some portion of their potential losses, even when perfect hedges are not available.

■ *Background.* Assume the same background as in Example 2 except that a perfect hedge is not available, although the firm expects that an available cross-hedge will be highly effective. For example, derivative contracts for the identical type of grain and delivery point may not be available, resulting in a less than perfect correlation between price changes in the underlyings of the derivative and those of the inventory being hedged. At year-end, the fair market value of the inventory is $565,000 lower, as in Example 2. The fair market value of the hedge, however, is only $510,000.

■ *Disclosure and financial analysis.* This example is illustrated in **Exhibit 5.3.** Assuming that management chooses, in this case, to offset the gain on the derivative contract directly against the loss in fair value of the inventory, the gross profit is $2,945,000 ($17,435,000 + $510,000 − $15,000,000). The decline in gross profit relative to that in Example 2 results from the mismatch of the derivative gain of $510,000 and the inventory fair market value loss of $565,000, or a $55,000 difference.

■ *Financial statement analysis implications.* The following summarizes the analysis and implications for a derivative (forward contract) used as a fair-value hedge of a commodity inventory immediately after the sale:

- This example makes clear that for fair-value hedges, all economic effects of both the hedge and the hedged item attributable to the hedged risk will flow together to the income statement every period. *The exact same accounting and reporting in the income statement would have been followed had the inventory not been sold and the derivative contracts not been closed out until the next period.* The cross-hedge is approximately 90 percent ($510,000/$565,000) effective in offsetting changes in the hedged item and could be considered to be highly effective. Recall that the FASB did not define "highly effective" in quantitative terms. Prior to SFAS No. 133, a rule of thumb for assessing whether a hedge was highly effective was to have a ratio between changes in the hedge and the hedged item of 80–120 percent. Gains and losses on the derivative flow to earnings each period in any case. Thus, application of the highly effective criterion only affects whether gains and losses on the hedging derivative can be matched by changes attributable to the same risk in the item hedged.

Exhibit 5.3. Statement Effects of Derivatives (Forward Contracts) Used to Hedge the Fair Market Value of a Commodity Inventory Immediately after Sale (with Ineffectiveness)

Assets =		Liabilities +	Equity	
Inventory	$18,000,000		Retained earnings	$ 2,945,000
Allowance to reduce value of inventory to market	(565,000)		Total	$ 2,945,000
Total	$17,435,000			
FMV of forward contract	510,000			
Total	$17,945,000			

	Income Statement	
Revenues		
Sales		$17,435,000
Gain on forward contract		510,000
Expenses		
Cost of goods sold		(15,000,000)
Gross Profit		$ 2,945,000
Other		
Net Income		$ 2,945,000

Note: In order to focus solely on derivative instrument effects, this example ignores effects of other transactions on the statements. Balance sheet at December 31, 2000.

• Because in this case management designated the derivative as a hedge of the entire value of the inventory (see Example 2 for the case in which the hedge is perfectly effective), the entire decline in the value of the inventory must be offset against the smaller gain on the derivative, even though the inventory had not been sold. Had management chosen to hedge only a portion of the risk, then that amount would have been matched against the derivative gain in the current period. This example emphasizes the importance placed on the details of the documentation linking the hedge to the item being hedged. Firms often hedge only about 50 percent of the risk in an item; SFAS No. 133 requires that this proportion be determined at the onset of the hedge and disclosed in the notes. One can now clearly see why this determination is important: Managers might otherwise have an incentive to determine the proportion hedged *ex post*—that is, after the gains and losses on the hedging instruments are known—in order to minimize earnings volatility. Strict application of the hedging criteria causes any hedging ineffectiveness to flow, without offset, to earnings immediately. Thus, managers have incentives to seek the most effective hedges if that is their intent in using the derivatives. In assessing hedge ineffectiveness, managers are permitted to exclude certain items, including the premium or discount on forward contracts, time value of the options, and the like. Kawaller and Koch (2000) discuss these and other problems involved in meeting the "highly effective expectation" criterion for hedge accounting.

- This example, as compared with Example 2, also illustrates the issue of earnings volatility—one of the more contentious questions raised during the exposure phase of SFAS No. 133. As Example 2 makes clear, no volatility is introduced into earnings if the hedge is perfectly effective. But if, as in this example, the hedge is less than 100 percent effective (a relatively common occurrence), then the *ineffectiveness* can result in volatility. For example, assume that instead of a gain on the derivative and a loss on the inventory, the situation had been reversed, with a gain on the inventory of $510,000 and a loss on the derivative of $565,000. The ultimate effect on earnings is the same (a loss of $55,000) compared with the results with a perfect hedge. The $55,000 must be recognized and introduces volatility. Again, managers have an incentive to seek highly effective hedges if such are available.

Example 4. Swap Used as a Fair-Value Hedge of Fixed-Rate Debt. As discussed in Chapter 2, interest rate swaps are the derivative instruments most commonly used by U.S. corporations at the present time. They are OTC contracts, and accounting for them in the past has been dependent on the cash inflows and outflows. Under SFAS No. 133, they are to be marked to market every period with gains and losses recognized currently. Managers may have a variety of reasons for engaging in swaps, but as this example illustrates, unless the swap has no ineffectiveness, volatility could be introduced into earnings.

■ *Background.* On January 1, 2000, TAP issues a $20,000,000 note at a fixed rate of 7 percent for six months to support short-term, floating-rate financing provided to its customers. At the end of the first quarter on March 31, TAP will make an interest payment of $350,000 ($20,000,000 × 0.07 × 1/4), and on June 30 another $350,000 in interest plus the principal redemption of $20,000,000 will be made.

On the same day (January 1, 2000), TAP's chief financial officer has arranged for the firm to enter into a six-month $20,000,000 notional principal receive fixed (6.50 percent)/pay floating (three-month London Interbank Offered Rate) interest rate swap with quarterly settlement in arrears. The swap is intended as a fair-value hedge of the fixed-rate debt issued to support floating-rate customer financing. On January 1, 2000, three-month LIBOR is 6.25

percent, so TAP is scheduled to receive $12,500 [(0.0650 − 0.0625) × 1/4 × $20,000,000] at the end of the quarter from its counterparty to the swap. The combined interest payment on the underlying note and the receipt on the swap is $337,500, which corresponds to a 6.75 percent cost of funds for the quarter and is equal to LIBOR plus 0.50 percent.

On March 31, three-month LIBOR turns out to be 7.25 percent. TAP is obligated to pay the swap counterparty $37,500 [(0.0650 − 0.0725) × 1/4 × $20,000,000] on June 30 at the termination of the agreement. For the second quarter, the combined payments on the note and the swap are $387,500, corresponding to a 7.75 percent cost of funds. Again, by design, that amount equals LIBOR plus 0.50 percent.

On March 31, the fair value of the swap is *negative* $36,787 [$37,500/(1 + 0.0775/4)]. That amount is the present value of the payment owed to the counterparty, discounted using TAP's three-month cost of borrowed funds. The fair value of the underlying note that has three months remaining until maturity is $19,963,213 [$20,350,000/(1 + 0.0775/4)]. The change in the fair value of the note (negative $36,787) matches exactly the change in the fair value of the swap because the terms of the note and the swap matched and, importantly, because there is no change in TAP's credit spread over LIBOR.

Because the critical terms of the swap and the note match, we have assumed that TAP has elected to use the shortcut method for assessing effectiveness. That is, the effect of the swap has been to convert the 7 percent fixed-rate note to floating rate at LIBOR plus 0.50 percent. In addition, all of the remaining important terms—the notional amount, maturity dates, and the like—are the same.

The financial statement effects of these transactions are shown in **Exhibit 5.4**. The bookkeeping entries for these transactions would be quite complex, involving, in addition to the items shown, accruals for interest receivable of $12,500 and interest payable of $350,000 in the balance sheet as well as the changes in the fair value of the swap and the note in the income statement, which directly offset. For simplicity, Exhibit 5.4 focuses on the main economic effects: the quarterly effect on cash, the fair value of the swap and the note in the balance sheet at the end of the quarter, and the net effect on income of the interest revenue of $12,500 and interest expense of $350,000. Similar transactions would be recorded on June 30.

▨ *Disclosure and financial analysis.* On TAP's March 31 financial statements, the $350,000 interest payment and the $12,500 receipt on the swap settlement are recorded as interest expense. Under SFAS No. 133, the negative $36,787 fair value of the swap must be reported on the balance sheet as a financial liability. That amount, however, is matched by the $36,787 reduction

Exhibit 5.4. Statement Effects of Derivatives (Swap Contracts) Used as a Fair-Value Hedge of a Liability at the End of the First Quarter

Assets =		Liabilities +		Shareholders' Equity	
Cash	$20,000,000	Notes payable	$19,963,213	Retained earnings	($337,500)
Less: Interest paid	(337,500)				
Total	$19,662,500				
Fair value of swap contract	(36,787)				
Total	$19,625,713	Total	$19,963,213	Total	($337,500)

	Income Statement	
	Revenues	
	Expenses	
	Other	
	Interest expense	($337,500)
	Net Income	($337,500)

Note: In order to focus solely on derivative instrument effects, this example ignores effects of other transactions on the statements. Balance sheet at March 31, 2000.

---

in the carrying value of the 7 percent fixed-rate note. Both of those amounts also go to equity through the income statement. In this example, there is no impact on earnings volatility because there was no ineffectiveness in the hedge.

If LIBOR had been below 6.50 percent on March 31, the swap would have had positive value to TAP. It would have appeared as a financial asset on the balance sheet, offsetting the increased carrying value of the underlying note. Those changes in fair value would have run through the income statement but still would not have introduced any volatility.

Because the notional principal of the pay-fixed debt and the receive-fixed swap are the same and the term to maturity is the same for each, there is no ineffectiveness in the swap. The net effect of the swap is to convert the 7 percent fixed-rate debt to floating rate at LIBOR plus 0.50 percent. Thus, instead of paying interest at the fixed annual rate of 7 percent (or $350,000 each quarter), TAP has arranged to pay the floating rate in effect at the beginning of each quarter plus 0.50 percent. Because the swap used as a fair-value hedge of the fixed-rate debt has no ineffectiveness, there will be no *net* balance sheet effects, and the sole *net* effect of the swap will be on interest expense in the income statement.

■ *Financial statement analysis implications.* The following summarizes the analysis and implications for a swap used as a fair-value hedge of fixed-rate debt:

- SFAS No. 133 permits the use of a "shortcut" accounting method for hedged items and the hedging swaps when the terms of each (including notional amount) are the same, the fair value of the swap at inception is zero, the method of computing the net settlement is the same for each settlement, and the hedged item is not prepayable. Put simply, all of the terms are the same. This allowance greatly simplifies the accounting and leads to a presumption of no ineffectiveness in the hedge.
- The general rationale for the swap in this example is that firms will generally borrow at the most favorable terms available to them, whether fixed or floating. Then, swaps may be used to transform the borrowings into the form that most clearly conforms to the firm's capital structure and risk management objectives. Under pre-SFAS No. 133 rules, so-called synthetic instrument accounting would have permitted the combination of the borrowing and the swap to be treated as a single entity for accounting purposes. Consequently, the debt typically would have been disclosed in the balance sheet and related schedules as floating-rate debt, possibly with some disclosure in the notes regarding any swap arrangements. SFAS No. 133, however, eliminates synthetic instrument accounting to preserve the concept of hedge accounting as the sum of two distinct elements: (1) the changes in the underlying of the hedged item and (2) the changes in the same underlying of the derivative used as a hedge. Thus, the two instruments and their effects must be disclosed separately in the financial statements.
- The concept of hedge accounting is important in analyzing the resulting financial statements because a logical disconnection seems to exist between the primary objectives for entering into the debt/swap arrangement and the hedge accounting followed for the derivative. The background in this example, which is based closely on an example provided in SFAS No. 133, clearly indicates that the intent is to better align the payments (cash outflows) on debt issued to support floating rate financing for customers (cash inflows). The stated reason for the hedge, to swap fixed-rate debt *issued to support floating-rate customer financing*, indicates that this is a cash flow hedge—a hedge of the volatility in future cash flows. That is, when a firm enters into an interest rate swap of the type described, a receive fixed/pay floating swap, the intent seems to be to "hedge" the future cash flows—perhaps in anticipation of an expected decline in interest rates or *to better match asset flows*, not to hedge the fair

value of the debt. First, the firm is obligated to the lender to repay the principal ($20,000,000), not more or less, at maturity, so there would appear to be no economic exposure to changes in the fair market value of the fixed-rate debt as interest rates change. Second, historical cost-basis accounting at present shows such debt in the balance sheet at the face amount ($20,000,000) regardless of market changes prior to maturity.[1]

Thus, there is no "accounting" exposure as might occur in the case of changes in currency exchange rates when consolidating foreign subsidiaries. The current fair market value of the debt is relevant only if the firm contemplates early extinguishment of the debt or if a full mark-to-market balance sheet is desired. Recall that if the swap qualifies as a hedge, then that portion of the debt hedged will be marked to fair value *for changes in the risk hedged*—interest rate risk in this case.

- As shown in Chapter 4, this same swap arrangement could have been treated as a cash flow hedge of the floating rate loans to customers. In this case, any gains or losses on the swap would have been recorded in comprehensive income in equity until matched by the corresponding cash flows on the debt, at which time the cash flows would be recycled into earnings. The derivative would have been recorded at fair value in the balance sheet; however, the debt would not have been marked to market. This result is most important for financial corporations that hold a significant amount of financial assets. Thus, management has substantial discretion under SFAS No. 133 in deciding not only the nature of hedging arrangements entered into but also what accounting should follow. *The clear implication for analysts is that attention will have to be given to the stated economic purposes for hedging transactions and to the way in which the hedges were accomplished; analysts cannot simply look to the accounting method chosen to interpret the statement disclosures.*

Example 5. Time Warner's Swap Used as a Fair-Value Hedge of Fixed-Rate Debt. This example illustrates the points made in the previous example under "Financial statement analysis implications." Time Warner (TW) was among the first firms to report under SFAS No. 133 prior to the extension of the required implementation date. (The date was extended in SFAS No. 137, *Accounting for Derivative Instruments and Hedging Activities— Deferral of the Effective Date of FASB Statement No. 133—an Amendment of FASB Statement No. 133,* by one year to June 15, 2000, to permit firms more time to address the reporting complexities and to make necessary revisions

---

[1]The FASB is currently studying issues surrounding the recording of fair market values of debt in the balance sheet, and new rules may be forthcoming.

to their accounting systems.) Thus, TW's statements and notes provide an early look at disclosures under the rule.

TW discloses in its 1998 10-K filing with the U.S. Securities and Exchange Commission (SEC) that the firm uses receive fixed/pay floating interest rate swaps as fair-value hedges of fixed-rate debt, similar to Example 4:

> Time Warner uses interest rate swap contracts to adjust the proportion of total debt that is subject to variable and fixed-interest rates. At December 31, 1998, Time Warner had interest rate swap contracts to pay floating rates of interest (average six-month LIBOR rate of 5.5 percent) and receive fixed rates of interest (average rate of 5.5 percent) on $1.6 billion notional amount of indebtedness, which resulted in approximately 37 percent of Time Warner's underlying debt, and 39 percent of the debt of Time Warner and the Entertainment Group combined, being subject to variable interest rates. At December 31, 1997, Time Warner had interest rate swap contracts on $2.3 billion notional amount of indebtedness. (p. 69, F-18)
>
> For interest rate swap contracts under which Time Warner agrees to pay variable rates of interest, these contracts are considered to be a hedge against changes in the fair value of Time Warner's fixed-rate debt obligations. Accordingly, the interest rate swap contracts are reflected at fair value in Time Warner's consolidated balance sheet and the related portion of fixed-rate debt being hedged is reflected at an amount equal to the sum of its carrying value plus an adjustment representing the change in fair value of the debt obligations attributable to the interest rate risk being hedged. In addition, changes during any accounting period in the fair value of these interest rate swap contracts, as well as offsetting changes in the adjusted carrying value of the related portion of the fixed-rate debt being hedged, are recognized as adjustments to interest expense in Time Warner's consolidated statement of operations. The net effect of this accounting on Time Warner's operating results is that interest expense on the portion of fixed-rate debt being hedged is generally recorded based on variable interest rates . . . . The net gain or loss on the ineffective portion of these interest rate swap contracts was not material in any period. (pp. 106–107, F-56)

A number of points are of interest:

- TW states that the intent is to adjust the relative proportions of fixed- and variable-rate debt, and no other reason is suggested, such as a need to better match asset and liability fair values. No additional insight is provided as to precisely why hedging the fair value of the debt is economically desirable. Thus, as with Example 4, the real focus here would seem to be more on the cash flows—that is, fixed versus variable— rather than on the fair values of the debt. But TW indicates that the pay-variable swap contracts are "considered to be" fair-value hedges.
- Assuming the notional amounts and other factors are the same, the gains and losses on the debt and the swap taken together should offset, and TW indicates that the ineffectiveness was "not material." Observe that TW would presumably be permitted to use the shortcut method under these conditions—that is, if the terms are the same.

- The gains and losses in fair value, along with the net amount of interest received or paid, are recorded in interest expense in the income statement. Thus, TW nets the sum of all of the effects of the debt and swaps in the same line item in the income statement, and it states that the net effect is to convert the fixed-rate debt to variable-rate debt. This treatment is strongly reminiscent of synthetic instrument accounting, which was eliminated under SFAS No. 133.

- Note that SFAS No. 133 provides an example of just such a receive fixed/pay-variable swap used as a fair-value hedge of fixed-rate debt, although the economic logic behind this example is not entirely transparent, as indicated in Example 4. PricewaterhouseCoopers provides insight on this accounting result:

  > . . . [t]he use of an interest rate swap to change nonprepayable (i.e., noncallable) fixed-rate debt into variable rate debt. (Although entities may not have viewed this strategy as a "fair-value" hedge of the fixed-rate debt, FAS 133 accommodates—in the income statement—the previous synthetic accounting practice of converting nonprepayable fixed-rate debt to variable rate debt by classifying that strategy as a fair-value hedge.) (PricewaterhouseCoopers 1998, p. 99)

Thus, the inevitable conclusion is that accounting for derivatives under SFAS No. 133 need not be driven by the economic motivation for entering into the derivative position, adjusting the cash flows in this case. Instead, the firm may look to the desired accounting treatment when selecting the type of hedge, for fair-value hedges in this case, which more closely approximates the former synthetic instrument accounting.

- Consequently, *analysts evaluating the statements and related notes with the goal of understanding the firm's risk positions, derivative use, management strategies, and the implications for the firm's future risk profiles and profitability will have to look well beyond the specific accounting method chosen to the apparent economics underlying the transactions. This assessment will be critically dependent on both the quality and quantity of disclosure that management chooses to provide.* To the extent that management is less than forthcoming, the analyst could be led to incorrect conclusions. Chapter 4 details SEC-required disclosures regarding firms' use of derivatives, and this information, combined with SFAS No. 133 data, may prove helpful in ascertaining the nature of firms' hedging and other derivative transactions and the extent of their use of derivatives. The basic questions the analyst should ask are outlined earlier in this chapter and will be discussed further in Chapter 6.

Cash Flow Hedges

Cash flow hedges are used to hedge exposure to cash flow volatility resulting from exposure to a *variable* market risk. Examples are loan receivables with floating-rate interest and future payments based on some, as yet indeterminate, variables, such as forecasted sales. To hedge a variable market risk, the cash flow hedge must, in effect, *fix* or "lock in" the terms of the item hedged. This effect is opposite to the one sought with a fair-value hedge, in which the objective is to release fixed terms. *A fair-value hedge, by releasing fixed terms, exposes the firm to the full range of favorable and unfavorable cash flow outcomes in order to protect the balance sheet. A cash flow hedge fixes the terms, removing exposure from cash flow variability but at a potential cost of balance sheet volatility.* A cash flow hedge may be used for the exposure of cash flows associated with a recognized existing asset, liability, or a forecasted (anticipated) transaction that is deemed to have a high probability of occurrence. The cash flows hedged cannot be from a firm commitment because their terms are, by definition, fixed and not subject to variability. Thus, firm commitments are required to be treated as fair-value hedges under SFAS No. 133.

Accounting for cash flow hedges requires that the following occur:

- The fair value of the derivative must be recorded in the balance sheet.
- The effective portion of the change in fair value of the derivative during the period must be recorded in other comprehensive income in shareholders' equity.
- The amount recorded in comprehensive income must be recycled into income and matched against the cash flows of the forecasted transaction when it is recognized.
- The ineffective portion of the derivative must be recognized currently in income.

Observe that with cash flow hedges, unlike with fair-value hedges, there will be no immediate matching of changes in the hedge instrument and the item hedged because the amount of change in the hedged item has, by definition, yet to be determined. This mismatch is the reason that the change in the derivative instrument is recorded in comprehensive income in equity until the hedged transaction is completed, at which time the derivative flows become eligible to be recycled into earnings and matched against the hedged cash flows. Consequently, for cash flow hedges, derivative gains or losses are accumulated and deferred outside earnings. Depending on the nature of the item hedged, earnings recognition of the derivative gain or loss might be delayed beyond the point at which the forecasted transaction is completed. For example, if the firm enters into a cash flow hedge for forecasted purchases of inventory, the derivative gain or loss must be recognized not when the inventory is finally purchased but when it is sold. Thus, recognition of derivative gains and losses might be delayed one or more periods as compared with fair-value hedges, for which they flow into earnings immediately.

Example 6. Derivative Used as a Hedge of Cash Flow Variability.

A firm may designate a derivative as a hedge of the exposure to cash flow variability in either an existing asset or liability or in a forecasted transaction, for example, anticipated sales, purchases, or debt issuances. Thus, the firm might desire to enter into a derivative contract that would effectively offset changes in cash flows in the hedged item.

Cash flow hedges are subject to qualifying criteria that have the effect of limiting the use of cash flow hedge treatment to certain types of items. In addition, a hedge of a forecasted transaction must be a single transaction or a group of individual transactions that share the same risk exposure. SFAS No. 133 also requires that the forecasted transaction hedged be probable, defined as "likely to occur." The probability of occurrence should be assessed by considering the frequency of similar past transactions, the ability of the firm to carry out the transaction, commitments of resources to the activity, the effect on operations if the transaction does not occur, the expected length of time until the transaction is expected to occur, and the quantity of the anticipated transactions.

   Background. Assume the same background as in Example 2. Recall that early in 2000, TAP enters into forward contracts to hedge one type of grain inventory, which had cost $15,000,000 to produce (that is, to grow, harvest, and process for storage), by selling contracts forward. The fair market value of the inventory is $18,000,000 on the contract trade date. The contracts extend beyond the current fiscal year and are for the exact same commodity as the inventory and delivered to the same geographical location. The notional principal of the forward contracts and the *fair market value* (which differs from cost by the profit margin) of the inventory hedged are the same ($18,000,000), and no premium is paid or received. The derivative qualifies for and is designated as a fair-value hedge of the inventory, and the firm intends for the derivative to hedge the entire gain or loss of the inventory. On the last day of 2000, the fiscal year-end, the derivative contracts have a fair value of $565,000 and the inventory has declined in fair value by $565,000. Management decides to sell the inventory and closes out the derivative contracts on that date.

In this example, however, assume that TAP wishes to hedge the anticipated cash flow variability of estimated future sales rather than the fair value of the commodity inventory. Such a hedge would be a relatively common hedge for a firm with large cross-border exposures.

82

■ *Disclosure and financial analysis.* Again, SFAS No. 133 makes clear through examples that the firm may designate the same hedge as either a fair-value or a cash flow hedge. The *interim* accounting, however, will differ depending on the type of hedge chosen. In this case, the accounting for the hedge will differ markedly from that in Example 2.

Just before the sale of the inventory on December 31, 2000, the effects on TAP's balance sheet and income statement of the cash flow hedge, ignoring tax effects and other items, would be similar to those shown in **Exhibit 5.5a**. Immediately after the sale of the inventory and closing out and settlement of the futures contracts, ignoring tax effects and other items, the effects on TAP's balance sheet and income statement of the cash flow hedge would be similar to those in **Exhibit 5.5b**.

■ *Financial statement analysis implications.* The following summarizes the analysis and implications for a derivative used as a hedge of cash flow variability:

- The change in the fair value of the derivative ($565,000) must be recorded in the balance sheet. But because it is designated as a cash flow hedge, not a fair-value hedge of an asset or liability, there is no offsetting change in fair value of the hedged item recorded before the sale and settlement of the contract.
- The change in the fair value of the forward contract (a gain of $565,000) is not recognized in earnings immediately but is recorded in comprehensive income, a component of shareholders' equity, until it is

Exhibit 5.5a. Statement Effects of Derivatives (Forward Contracts) Used as a Cash Flow Hedge of a Commodity Inventory Immediately before the Sale of the Inventory and Closing of the Contract

Assets =		Liabilities +	Equity	
Forward contract	$565,000		Other comprehensive income	$565,000
			Retained earnings	0
Total	$565,000		Total	$565,000
			Income Statement	
			Revenues	
			Expenses	
			Other	
			Net Income	$ 0

Note: In order to focus solely on derivative instrument effects, this example ignores effects of other transactions on the statements. Balance sheet at December 31, 2000.

Exhibit 5.5b. Statement Effects of Derivatives (Forward Contracts) Used as a Cash Flow Hedge of a Commodity Inventory Immediately after Sale and Settlement of the Forward Contract

Assets =		Liabilities +	Equity	
Cash	$3,000,000		Other comprehensive income	$ 0
			Retained earnings	3,000,000
Total	$3,000,000		Total	$ 3,000,000
			Income Statement	
			Revenues	
			Sales	$17,435,000
			Gain on forward contract	565,000
			Expenses	
			Cost of goods sold	(15,000,000)
			Gross Profit	$ 3,000,000
			Other	
			Net Income	$ 3,000,000

Note: In order to focus solely on derivative instrument effects, this example ignores effects of other transactions on the statements. Balance sheet at December 31, 2000.

---

matched against the cash flows of the hedged item; then, the gain will be recycled into earnings in the income statement and into retained earnings in shareholders' equity.

- *Although the background of this example is identical to that in Example 2, designation of the forward contract by TAP as a hedge of the cash flow variability of the future sale of the inventory, rather than as a fair-value hedge of the inventory, results in deferral of the gain on the derivative until the cash flows are realized from the sale of the inventory. Thus, again, the accounting designation of the nature of the hedge, which rests largely with the discretion of management, produces widely different interim balance sheet and income statement effects. But regardless of how accrual accounting accounts for and discloses transactions in the interim, if the economic nature—that is, the cash flows—are the same, the ultimate general effects of the transaction on the balance sheet and income statement must be the same.* Observe that in Example 2 and here in Example 6, both the risk hedged and the hedging instrument are the same; merely the accrual accounting designation of the hedge is different. The analyst will recall from basic accounting that cash flows are unaffected by accrual accounting, although the classifications (locations) of the cash flows reported in the cash flow statement may be different depending on the specific accrual designation of the transaction. As a consequence, the ultimate effects on assets, liabilities, shareholders' equity, and income must be the same if the transaction is the same, as it was in this case. The interim effects, however, can be substantially different. Certainly, if the transactions hedged were different or different hedging strategies were used, then the final effects would not be identical.

- Note that deferral of the gain on the cash flow hedge in other comprehensive income, recorded in shareholders' equity, results in a "recycling" of the same gain to income and retained earnings when the cash flows are matched. This recycling effect was widely discussed prior to the issuance of SFAS No. 133. Currently, several other items result in the same treatment under SFAS No. 130, *Reporting Comprehensive Income*, including some foreign currency translation adjustments in consolidation of foreign subsidiaries and gains and losses on available-for-sale securities when the securities are sold. The role of other comprehensive income is to capture as yet unrealized gains and losses that could be expected to affect earnings in a future period.

Example 7: Time Warner's Use of a Derivative as a Hedge of Cash Flow Variability. One of the examples provided in SFAS No. 133 relates to interest rate swaps designated as cash flow hedges of variable rate liabilities. The example indicates that receive floating/pay fixed swaps may be designated as hedges of the cash flow variability in variable rate debt. The swap has the effect of converting variable- to fixed-rate liabilities.

Time Warner reports the following in Note 15 in its 1998 10-K:

Time Warner accounts for its interest rate swap contracts differently, based on whether it has agreed to pay an amount based on a variable rate or fixed-rate of interest. . . . For interest rate swap contracts under which Time Warner agrees to pay fixed-rates of interest, these contracts are considered to be a hedge against changes in the amount of future cash flows associated with Time Warner's interest payments of Time Warner's variable rate debt obligations. Accordingly, the interest rate swap contracts are reflected at fair value in Time Warner's consolidated balance sheet and the related gains or losses on these contracts are deferred in shareholders' equity (as a component of comprehensive income). These deferred gains and losses are then amortized as an adjustment to interest expense over the same period in which the related interest payments being hedged are recognized in income. However, to the extent that any of these contracts are not considered to be perfectly effective in offsetting the change in the value of the interest payments being hedged, any changes in fair value relating to the ineffective portion of these contracts are immediately recognized in income. The net effect of this accounting on Time Warner's operating results is that interest expense on the portion of the variable rate debt being hedged is generally recorded based on fixed interest rates. (p. 107, F-56)

Time Warner's disclosure of derivative financial instrument losses recorded in other comprehensive income in the 10-K reveals that $38 million of losses were recorded, all of them incurred in 1998, of which $32 million was associated with another strategy.

■ *Financial statement analysis implications.* The following summarizes the analysis and implications of Time Warner's use of a derivative as a hedge of cash flow variability:

- Note that by converting a portion of the debt from variable rate to fixed rate, TW exposes the debt to changes in fair value, which would have to be recognized in both the balance sheet and the income statement were the hedges to be treated as fair-value hedges. Indeed, TW discloses in its 1998 10-K in Note 7:

  > Based on the level of interest rates prevailing at December 31, 1998 and 1997, the fair value of Time Warner's fixed-rate debt exceeded its carrying value by $1.098 billion and $753 million, respectively. Unrealized gains or losses on debt do not result in the realization or expenditure of cash and generally are not recognized for financial reporting purposes, unless the debt is retired prior to its maturity. (p. 97, F-46)

  The increases in fair value of the debt are a result of lower interest rates on the debt. Note that if these were to be recognized, the "gains" in debt would result in losses in the income statement. But because the net pay fixed hedges are designated as cash flow hedges, any gains or losses on the hedged items are not recognized. The gains and losses on the hedging instrument, however, are recorded both in the balance sheet and in other comprehensive income.

- A careful comparison of this example with Example 5 (Time Warner's disclosure of its use of receive fixed/pay-variable swaps as fair-value hedges) indicates that the accounting method chosen for the instruments in each case results in the minimal effect on the statements of the disclosure. Sufficient latitude is available to firms in choosing between fair-value and cash flow hedges under SFAS No. 133 to permit management to select the method that will provide the desired effect. Given the observation above that the fair value of the hedged liabilities in both cases exceeded the book or face value, indicating a reduction in the effective interest rate of the obligations as a result of the hedging transactions, *an analyst could conclude that the primary motivation of the firm in using the derivatives was to reduce borrowing costs, not merely to hedge cash flow volatility or fair-value exposure per se. Obviously, reduction of borrowing costs or hedging cash flow volatility could provide a real economic benefit to the firm, a most important point for an analyst but one that is obscured by the complexity of the accounting.* But because the firm does not address this issue, one cannot automatically assume it to be the case. An analyst might well seek additional information from TW regarding its hedging strategy and motivations for both the fair-value and cash flow swaps.

- The economics of the transaction in this example would seem to be better reflected in the use of the cash flow hedge rather than in the treatment used in Example 5, a fair-value hedge designation for the pay-variable swap, where the fair value does not appear to be exposed to market risk.

- In general, conversion of variable-rate assets and liabilities to a fixed rate exposes them to fair-value market risk while reducing cash flow variability, whereas the conversion to variable rates reduces fair-value exposures at the cost of increasing cash flow volatility. Thus, a trade-off needs to be made. In Example 5, recall that TW did not have any discernible fair-value exposure with the fixed-rate debt, unless the firm chose to extinguish the debt early. The hedges, however, were designated as fair-value hedges, hence the PricewaterhouseCoopers observation that these transactions would not usually be thought of as fair-value hedges.

Derivatives Used as Foreign Currency Hedges

Derivatives used as foreign currency hedges may be used to hedge the exposure of unrecognized firm commitments, available-for-sale securities, foreign-currency-denominated forecasted transactions, and net investments in foreign operations.

Accounting for these items may be described briefly as follows:

- Hedges of unrecognized firm commitments must be treated as fair-value hedges and accounted for as outlined in the section of this chapter titled "Fair-Value Hedges." (Nonderivative instruments may be used as hedges for this class of item, an exception to SFAS No. 133's general hedge model.)

- SFAS No. 138, *Accounting for Certain Derivative Instruments and Certain Hedging Activities—an Amendment of FASB Statement No. 133,* permits hedge accounting for foreign-currency-denominated (exposed) balance sheet items, primarily receivables and payables—a change from SFAS No. 133.

- Hedges of available-for-sale securities must be treated as fair-value hedges, but the hedge must be a derivative instrument.

- Hedges of foreign-currency-denominated forecasted transactions must be treated as cash flow hedges and reported and disclosed as in the previous section "Cash Flow Hedges."

- Hedges of the net investment in foreign operations follow the accounting prescribed in SFAS No. 52, *Foreign Currency Translation,* regarding translation of foreign-currency-denominated statements; that is, the change in fair value of the derivative (a nonderivative hedging instrument may be used) must be reported in the same manner as the gain or loss in translation, generally as an adjustment to the cumulative translation adjustment account in shareholders' equity. *Importantly, the gain or loss on the derivative must not be recognized in earnings, another exception to SFAS No. 133's general hedge accounting model.*

Example 8. Time Warner's Foreign Currency Risk Management. Time Warner discloses the use of foreign exchange currency sale and purchase contracts to hedge exposures to a variety of currencies. Information regarding the contracts is provided in Time Warner's 1998 10-K in the Notes to Consolidated Financial Statements:

> Foreign exchange contracts are used primarily by Time Warner to hedge the risk that unremitted or future royalties and license fees owed to Time Warner or TWE [Time Warner Entertainment, a subsidiary of TW] domestic companies for the sale or anticipated sale of U.S. copyrighted products abroad may be adversely affected by changes in foreign currency exchange rates. As part of its overall strategy to manage the level of exposure to the risk of foreign currency exchange rate fluctuations, Time Warner hedges a portion of its and TWE's combined foreign currency exposures anticipated over the ensuing 12-month period. At December 31, 1998, Time Warner had effectively hedged approximately half of the combined estimated foreign currency exposures that principally relate to anticipated cash flows to be remitted to the United States over the ensuing 12-month period. To hedge this exposure, Time Warner used foreign exchange contracts that generally have maturities of three months or less, which generally will be rolled over to provide continuing coverage throughout the year. Time Warner often closes foreign exchange sale contracts by purchasing an offsetting purchase contract. Time Warner reimburses or is reimbursed by TWE for contract gains and losses related to TWE's foreign currency exposure. Foreign currency contracts are placed with a number of major financial institutions in order to minimize credit risk.
>
> Time Warner records these foreign exchange contracts at fair value in its consolidated balance sheet and the related gains or losses on these contracts are deferred in shareholders' equity (as a component of comprehensive income). These deferred gains and losses are recognized in income in the period in which the related royalties and license fees being hedged are received and recognized in income. However, to the extent that any of these contracts are not considered to be perfectly effective in offsetting the change in the value of the royalties and license fees being hedged, any changes in fair value relating to the ineffective portion of these contracts are immediately recognized in income. Gains and losses on foreign exchange contracts are generally included as a component of interest and other, net, in Time Warner's consolidated statement of operations.

At December 31, 1998, Time Warner had contracts for the sale of $755 million and the purchase of $259 million of foreign currencies at fixed rates, primarily Japanese yen (40 percent of net contract value), English pounds (4 percent), German marks (28 percent), Canadian dollars (10 percent) and French francs (16 percent), compared to contracts for the sale of $507 million and the purchase of $139 of foreign currencies at December 31, 1997. Time Warner had deferred approximately $6 million of net losses on foreign exchange contracts at December 31, 1998, which is all expected to be recognized in income over the next 12 months. For the years ended December 31, 1998, 1997, and 1996, Time Warner recognized $8 million in losses, $27 million in gains, and $15 million in gains, respectively, and TWE recognized $2 million in losses, $14 million in gains, and $6 million in gains, respectively, on foreign exchange contracts, which were or are expected to be offset by corresponding decreases and increases, respectively, in the dollar value of foreign currency royalties and license fee payments that have been or are anticipated to be received in cash from the sale of U.S. copyrighted products abroad. (p. 108, F-57)

A close reading of Time Warner's disclosure indicates that both types of hedged items—that is, "unremitted" and "anticipated" royalties and license fees owed to Time Warner—are treated as cash flow hedges in the balance sheet and income statement with the fair value of the derivatives recorded in the balance sheet and the gain or loss deferred in other comprehensive income in shareholders' equity, to be recycled into income when the unremitted or anticipated royalties and license fees are recognized. Thus, one can assume that the unremitted items do not qualify as firm commitments, which must be recorded as fair-value hedges.

Observe that Time Warner generated large gains from the contracts in 1997 and 1996, which, presumably, offset large transaction foreign exchange losses. In 1998, the losses recognized currently on the contracts amounted to $8 million with an additional $6 million of losses deferred in comprehensive income. All of the amounts represent a significant amount of reported earnings in these years. Thus, one can assume that Time Warner has a relatively large exposure to foreign currency risk from its foreign sales and operations. Moreover, Time Warner has chosen to hedge only about half of its estimated foreign currency exposure, according to the note.

SEC Derivative Risk Disclosure Guidelines

The SEC has disclosure requirements that complement the FASB's SFAS No. 133 disclosures. The primary objective of the SEC's requirements is to focus on risk exposures inherent in a firm's derivative strategies. In contrast, SFAS No. 133, consistent with accounting practice, deals with information regarding *existing or current positions, gains, and losses and does not require information concerning potential future effects of these positions and strategies on a firm's operations and financial condition.* Consequently, these disclosures can be particularly useful to analysts in assessing firms' risk *exposures* compared with current risk *positions*.

Firms are given substantial latitude under the current rules for reporting these risks. As shown briefly in Chapter 4, the SEC requires, in addition to qualitative information, that firms use one of three methods for conveying potential risks:

- tables showing notional amounts and related gains or losses on derivative instruments;
- sensitivity analyses of the risk exposures; or
- value-at-risk analyses of risk exposures.

Based on the 10-K disclosures of a number of firms for 1998 and 1997, sensitivity analysis appears to be the method of choice, although all three methods have been used.

Example 9. Time Warner's SEC Derivative Risk Exposure Disclosures.
As observed above, Time Warner has chosen to hedge only about half of its projected foreign currency exposure to anticipated transactions. Further light is shed on the extent of Time Warner's exposure in its 1998 10-K disclosures, which use the sensitivity analysis format, found in the Management Discussion and Analysis of Results of Operations and Financial Condition, as required by SEC disclosure rules rather than those of SFAS No. 133:

> Based on the foreign exchange contracts outstanding at December 31, 1998, each 5 percent devaluation of the U.S. dollar, as compared to the level of foreign exchange rates for currencies under contract at December 31, 1998, would result in approximately $38 million of unrealized losses and $13 million of unrealized gains on foreign exchange contracts involving foreign currency sales and purchases, respectively. Conversely, a 5 percent appreciation of the U.S. dollar would result in $38 million of unrealized gains and $13 million of unrealized losses, respectively. With regard to the net $25 million of unrealized losses or gains on foreign exchange contracts, Time Warner would be reimbursed by TWE, or would reimburse TWE, respectively, for approximately $10 million, net, related to TWE's foreign currency exposure. Consistent with the nature of the economic hedge provided by such foreign exchange contracts, such unrealized gains or losses would be offset by corresponding decreases or increases, respectively, in the dollar value of future foreign currency royalty and license fee payments that would be received in cash within the ensuing 12-month period from the sale of U.S. copyrighted products abroad. (p. 69, F-19)

This disclosure reinforces the observation that Time Warner has significant foreign currency exposure relative to earnings. If the contracts are, as Time Warner suggests, highly effective in offsetting exposures in anticipated transactions, then the effect is to dampen volatility in earnings arising from the exposure. The fact that Time Warner has entered contracts on a number of currencies, with a wide range of volatilities relative to the U.S. dollar, is interesting because the degree of risk exposure varies considerably between the currencies.

Summary

SFAS No. 133 is among the most complex and far-reaching accounting rules to date. Much of the complexity is a direct result of the nature of the transactions themselves. SFAS No. 133, however, also has adopted as a cardinal principle the recording of all derivatives in the balance sheet at fair market value, a major focus of all accounting rule making at present. This standard places relevance of information and timeliness of financial reporting above other accounting principles. Fair market value accounting results in periodic recognition of gains and losses, most of which will now be reported in periodic income. Thus, under SFAS No. 133, income will better reflect the economic changes in the value of the firm during the period.

Fair market value accounting, as compared with historical cost-basis accounting, requires extensive and detailed analysis, recording, and reporting. Moreover, the valuations and resulting gains and losses must be updated every reporting period. These changes have required substantial revision of existing accounting systems by all users of derivative instruments. Nonetheless, the gains in transparency of transactions, comparability across firms, and quality of information available both to users of derivative instruments and to analysts reviewing firms' performance should substantially outweigh the additional cost and effort.

Unfortunately, details of disclosures regarding income statement treatment of gains and losses on derivative contracts, with the exception of those resulting from hedging ineffectiveness, are not required, thus significantly reducing the transparency of derivative reporting in income.

6. Conclusion: SFAS No. 133 and Its Significance for Financial Analysis

Chapters 2–5 have provided general background on the issues of risk analysis and risk management and a summary of the implications of Statement of Financial Accounting Standards (SFAS) No. 133, *Accounting for Derivative Instruments and Hedging Activities*, that are of interest to the financial analyst. Although the principal objective of this concluding chapter is to integrate the earlier material into a useful framework for the working financial analyst, most analysts will have a better understanding of the problems and opportunities that SFAS No. 133 and the rise of risk management create for them if they focus, at least briefly, on the development of accounting policy in the United States.

Development of Accounting Policy and SFAS No. 133

What began in 1986 as the Financial Accounting Standards Board (FASB) project on financial instruments led to the release of SFAS No. 133 in June 1998. The principal FASB publication on SFAS No. 133 is a 245-page document consisting of 540 "paragraphs" detailing the requirements of SFAS No. 133, the rationale behind the specific decisions reached, and specific guidance for implementation.[1] The pages of the document are approximately textbook size, margins are narrow, and the nine-point type seems tightly packed. As a useful approximation, the text in the SFAS No. 133 publication is equivalent to more than two full issues of the *Financial Analysts Journal*. In short, this is a book— a longer and more complex book than some financial texts. The length of the book is partly the result of a detailed discussion of FASB's rationale for some controversial choices and a rather clear picture of how SFAS No. 133 is a transition document in the long-term development of accounting policy.[2]

The SFAS No. 133 "book" has a clear and useful table of contents but, unfortunately, no index. Appendix C, "Background Information and Basis for

---

[1]See Financial Accounting Standards Board (1998a).

[2]In addition, the FASB, the Derivatives Implementation Group, and most accounting firms have added generously to the available material on SFAS No. 133.

Conclusions," accounts for nearly half the volume and is essential reading for any analyst seeking to place SFAS No. 133 in an appropriate accounting policy development context. This appendix describes the FASB's ongoing efforts to move from what it has long referred to as the "mixed attribute accounting model" to something closely approximating a fair-value or market value model. Notwithstanding the dislocations of such a transition and intractable legal and regulatory obstacles to full realization of fair- or market value accounting, the FASB embraces the increasing availability of market valuations for most corporate assets and liabilities.

Even when a precise market value is not available for a particular instrument, contract, or miscellaneous asset or liability, close proxies and accepted evaluation methods are increasingly available to make a market value accounting system not only more useful if implemented but also far more practical then it has ever been before. A greater range of assets and liabilities are traded in the marketplace than have ever been traded before. The history of recent FASB pronouncements has been a history of increasing the use of frequently updated fair values and reducing the use of historical or book values for carrying assets and liabilities and calculating earnings. In each stage of this movement toward fair values in accounting for assets, liabilities, and earnings, the FASB has studied and updated its position on the availability of fair-value information on financial instruments and has promoted a steady shift from book value to market value. SFAS No. 133, the most recent major step in this transition, relies on the market values available for essentially all derivative instruments, but it still suffers from limitations that inhibit a full transition to fair-value accounting. Regulatory limitations—particularly for financial intermediaries with demand deposit liabilities and for insurance companies with long-dated liabilities—will continue to make market value accounting a difficult policy to implement fully, even in the very long term. A few of the issues the FASB has been wrestling with are best illustrated by comparing the hedge accounting rules under SFAS No. 133 with traditional hedge accounting.

New Paradigm for Hedge Accounting

One of the stated requirements for hedge accounting has always been that it demonstrate a high degree of effectiveness in matching the hedging instrument with the risk it hedges. Although approaches vary, this requirement has generally meant that the relationship between the risk being hedged and the hedging instrument should fall within the range of 80–120 percent of price movement. Few hedges were criticized if they met this relatively simple test in an era when fair-value information was less widely available than it is today. Without good price information, a hedging policy for which it was difficult to prove that it met even this simple test of effectiveness was often accepted. In the pre-SFAS No. 133 era, any slippage in the effectiveness of the hedge had no effect on the balance sheet or income statement until its ineffectiveness was clearly established or one or both sides of the hedge was closed out.

SFAS No. 133 complicates and sharpens evaluation of the hedging process dramatically in nearly every case. It requires that any evidence of ineffectiveness (with minimal exceptions) be funneled through earnings per share (EPS). Although SFAS No. 133 does offer a shortcut method to determine that some hedges are prima facie effective, any hedge that cannot meet the strict requirements of the shortcut method is marked to market though EPS. Furthermore, SFAS No. 133 makes implementing a macro hedge to reduce several risk factors at the same time practically impossible. Under SFAS No. 133, a specific hedging instrument must focus on a single class or category of risk or, at most, on related risks. The separation of risks to be hedged and the limitations on classes of risk that can be hedged make the hedging process more precise. Hedging can still reduce selected risk exposures, but any hedging failures are reflected in the financial statements in the period when the failure occurs. The new approach is much less forgiving than traditional hedge accounting.[3]

Changes in Earnings Stability and Comparability

SFAS No. 133, earlier FASB guidance on derivatives, and derivative disclosure required by the U.S. Securities and Exchange Commission (SEC) have complicated risk reporting and analysis without a clear increase in the usefulness of the information provided to most users of financial statements. The combination of new requirements plus the inevitably growing complexity of financial instruments and risk management applications have led to more disclosure—but not necessarily to better or more useful disclosure.

Many corporate financial officers and a number of analysts expect to see an "artificial" volatility increase in periodic corporate EPS reports.[4] Their expectations are grounded on the reasonable assumption that accounting changes, which introduce a number of essentially random positive or negative adjustments to EPS, increase earnings volatility.

Some increase in earnings volatility seems inevitable, but we suspect that this concern has been overblown. As Examples 2 and 6 in Chapter 5 indicate, by choosing carefully between fair-value hedges and cash flow hedges when practical (and recognizing that any transaction involving a corporation's own equity securities has no effect on earnings), the EPS volatility impact of the

---

[3]For more detail, see Chapter 4 and Kawaller and Koch (2000).

[4]See, for example, Louis (2000) and Reiner (2000).

new requirements can be relatively modest. SFAS No. 133 does introduce an element of random earnings variability, but financial corporations have used mark-to-market accounting for many purposes for years without major earnings concerns. For nonfinancial corporations, these random variations are likely to have no more than a marginal impact on reported EPS.

Although variability and unpredictability of corporate earnings are unlikely to reach the levels predicted by most of the FASB's critics, there is no question that the to-the-penny predictability of earnings, which has been the pride of some corporate financial divisions, will be a thing of the past for most firms with significant exposure to the requirements of SFAS No. 133. Thus, there will be a greater variable element in both the official corporate earnings estimate and analysts' forecasts of earnings.

Of greater concern than earnings fluctuations is an inevitable decline in comparability of financial statements among firms in the same industry and across industries. Although pinpointing a single development responsible for initiating this decline in reporting comparability is difficult, one culprit might be the SEC's disclosure requirements for corporate use of derivatives. Rather than mandate a single disclosure technique, the SEC offers derivative users a variety of ways to report their derivative positions and applications. For example, firms can provide relatively detailed tabular disclosure of the derivative instruments they held for various purposes, listing the characteristics of each instrument or of instruments in appropriate groupings. Alternatively, they can use some variation of value at risk (VAR) to disclose their expected risk of loss under a set of assumptions that they spell out for users of their financial reports. A third disclosure option is a scenario or sensitivity analysis designed to show the impact on financial results from relevant changes in key economic variables, such as interest rates, prices of one or more commodities, and so on. Appropriately, to date, the predominant reporting choice has been sensitivity analysis, but much less standardization exists than a more definitive requirement would have encouraged.

SFAS No. 133 promises to diversify financial reporting of hedging and derivatives even further. To illustrate how SFAS No. 133 encourages diversity, we quote—in its entirety—paragraph 506 of the SFAS No. 133 book. This paragraph describes the FASB's effort to reduce the cost of SFAS No. 133 disclosures by eliminating certain earlier proposals that were designed to encourage comparability:

> 506. In response to comments about the volume of the proposed disclosure requirements in both the exposure draft and the task force draft, the Board reconsidered the costs and benefits of the proposed disclosures. In reconsidering the proposed disclosures, the Board concluded that by eliminating certain of the requirements, it could reduce the cost of applying the Statement without significant reduction in the benefits to users. Consequently, the following proposed disclosures were eliminated:

a. Amount of gains and losses on hedged items and on related derivatives recognized in earnings for fair value hedges.

b. Description of where in the financial statements hedged items and the gains and losses on those hedged items are reported.

c. Cumulative net unamortized amount of gains and losses included in the carrying amount of hedged items.

d. Separate amounts for the reporting period of hedging gains and hedging losses on derivatives not recognized in earnings for cash flow hedges.

e. Description of where derivatives related to cash flow hedges are reported in the statement of financial position.

f. Separate amounts for the reporting period of gains and losses on the cash flow hedging instrument.

g. Amount of gains and losses recognized during the period on derivatives not designated as hedges.

h. Beginning and ending balances in accumulated other comprehensive income for accumulated derivative gains and losses, and the related current period changes, separately for the following two categories: (1) gains and losses related to forecasted transactions for which the variability of hedged future cash flows has ceased and (2) gains and losses related to forecasted transactions for which that variability has not ceased.

i. Description of where gains and losses on derivatives not designated as hedges are reported in the statement of income or other statement of financial performance.

In addition, the Board replaced some of the remaining proposed disclosures requiring separate amounts of gains and losses with disclosures requiring the amount of net gain or loss. (pp. 217–218)

Many of these items are unimportant, but others illustrate an undesirable lack of consistency more than desirable flexibility. More importantly, all these data are generated as part of the financial accounting process, and the cost of fuller and fully consistent reporting of most of these details should be nominal. Thanks to the relaxation of disclosure consistency reflected in Paragraph 506, obtaining reasonable comparability for some balance sheet or income statement ratio analyses requires a Herculean effort by any single analyst attempting to develop comparable data among the major firms in an industry, let alone among all U.S. firms publishing financial statements. We can only hope that over time, one advantage of the reduction in the number of major accounting firms may be some consistency of policy in reporting the periodic impact of the provisions of SFAS No. 133. One or more database firms will undoubtedly try to provide raw material for consistent financial analysis based on SFAS No. 133 requirements. The data digestion that this move toward consistency will permit should make the analyst's job more manageable. Unless further guidance from the FASB or the Derivatives Implementation Group is forthcoming, a period of uncertainty and confusion will exist as a result of so few requirements for comparability in terms of where items appear and how they are categorized.

Derivative Policy and Risk Management under SFAS No. 133

FASB reporting requirements, like the requirements of any regulator, develop partly as a response to past activities of regulated organizations. As with defense planners, a regulator is always fighting the previous war. Inappropriate uses of derivatives and inadequate reporting (based on inadequate understanding) of risk and risk management are the dominant causes of the changes wrought by SFAS No. 133, other recent FASB statements, and the SEC derivative disclosure requirements. The financial community needs to work its way through the temporary inconsistencies and dislocations that these disclosure and reporting requirements are creating. The pressure on corporate management to control the risk management process and to use derivatives more carefully has been well-intended and has led to closer examination of key corporate policies and to more intelligent risk management using derivatives. Getting to the present position has been awkward, and both analysts and reporting firms might wish the FASB had combined some of the steps on the road to general adoption of a fair-value accounting model in order to get there in fewer stages. Paragraph 506 alone adds more complexity than is justified by the limited increase in clarity and usefulness that all of SFAS No. 133 achieves. SFAS No. 133 is not "The Accounting Standard from Outer Space,"[5] but one can understand the basis for such a comment.

Risk Management and the Financial Analyst

Several results of the past few years' developments in corporate use of derivatives and changes in financial disclosure and reporting seem inevitable and noncontroversial. First, risk management is increasingly important to corporations, and more specifically, to the corporate treasury and financial management functions. A corollary of this point is that managers will have to understand risks and risk management more clearly than they have in the past, which does not mean that the typical general manager, or even the typical financial officer, needs a master's degree in mathematics to survive. It does mean, however, that managers involved in the risk management function will have to be able to communicate with other managers, and all managers will have to understand risk management issues and the basics of the risk management process.

A second result of recent developments is that there is likely to be a market valuation premium for firms that succeed in communicating sound risk and risk management policies to creditors, shareholders, and other constituents. One of the instruments of this communication is the financial analyst who

---

[5]See Hunter (1999).

follows the firm for its investors. Managers will have to communicate effectively with this analyst, and the analyst will have to have a clear understanding of the risk issues and the ability to answer questions posed by investors who lack the inclination or patience to read the financial statement footnotes or interview the corporate risk manager.

The Risk Management Interview

Almost inevitably, a new stop on the financial analyst's tour of top and middle management officers will be an interview with the corporate risk manager. In some firms, this function will be assigned to more than one individual or group. To the extent that the risks are principally financial or timing issues, the risk management function will probably be located on the financial side of the organization. To the extent that commodity exposure is extensive or risks are unusual in some respect, various parts of the operating organization may be involved.

The analyst needs to understand the firm's risk management objectives. Which risks are to be managed, and which are to be accepted? Formal risk management statements are more likely to be boilerplate than a useful statement of objectives, placing a premium on the ability to delve behind such policy statements. A comparison of the inventory of natural risks with the risks hedged and the risks accepted may highlight cases in which management is taking a risk that would be easily and appropriately hedged or is hedging an exposure that stockholders are holding the stock to obtain. An example of the latter might be gold producers who hedge away their exposure to gold price changes for a number of years into the future as described in Tufano (1996).

One important issue for the analyst is the relevance and quality of the risk management function. In the aftermath of the mid-1990s (i.e., the derivative problems described in Chapter 3), it became an article of faith that the risk management organization must be independent and report directly to the board of directors.[6] A number of firms have taken this prescription to heart and have adopted such a policy. Others, however, have taken the view that risk management is simply another staff function and most logically belongs in a staff division. Commonly, risk management becomes the chief financial officer's responsibility. The outside analyst will have to evaluate the safety and functionality of the risk management structure decisions that individual firms make. Independence of the risk manager is probably most important in a financial intermediary and least important where financial risk

---

[6]See Jorion (1997, pp. 299–304) and publications from many accounting firms for lists of "Best Practices" in risk management.

management is substantially less likely to have an impact on the balance sheet and income statement, as in a nonfinancial corporation. The analyst needs to ask the necessary series of pertinent and impertinent questions to gather the data and impressions to evaluate the risk management structure and the qualifications of the risk manager(s).

As recently as a few years ago, a key responsibility of most corporate risk managers was to see that the firm's fire insurance premiums were paid. Today's risk manager faces more challenging tasks. In addition to technical competence, the risk manager must understand the economics of the firm's business as thoroughly as any member of top management. This understanding must span a broader range of business and economic issues than an earlier generation of top management had to face.

The qualifications for an ideal risk manager read like the qualifications for the chief executive officer (CEO), with the risk manager needing more familiarity with quantitative tools than most CEOs can claim. A technically competent risk manager or risk management team needs business process and corporate structure knowledge, which are integral to effective corporate risk management. The depth of business knowledge that an effective risk manager needs can come only from on-the-job experience, and a substantial premium exists for being a quick study.

The typical pattern of hiring relatively inexperienced, but technically qualified, risk managers is obviously at odds with the experience and business knowledge requirement. If relationships between line managers and risk managers are good, the line manager's experience and the risk manager's technical expertise can be an awesome combination. Conversely, an adversarial relationship between risk management and line management will be destructive. Financial analysts will profit by being alert to the state of this critical relationship.

The analyst needs to evaluate the capabilities of the risk management staff for communicating the pertinent risk issues and ways of dealing with them. Apart from technical competence, the risk management organization must have the ability to communicate effectively on a variety of issues with its principal constituencies—top management and the board of directors. The analyst might want to question the risk manager in depth about one or more issues that determine the firm's risk management policies. Apart from the substance of the questions and answers, the analyst will be evaluating the quality of the interviewee's communication skills.

The analyst need not know a great deal about the specific tools of the risk manager or about higher mathematics to conduct a useful interview with a risk manager. But an effective risk manager has to be able to explain what the risk management group is doing and what tools it uses to the firm's staff and line management and to outside directors. If the analyst does not understand and accept the risk management process that the interviewee describes, the odds are high that the risk manager is not making his or her case to colleagues and that his or her efforts have little impact on management decisions.

Value at Risk

A limited exception to the principle that the analyst need not learn about risk management tools from the risk manager is VAR. All analysts who follow financial firms and most analysts who cover other firms should be thoroughly familiar with the strengths and weaknesses of major variations of the VAR methodology before they begin to evaluate corporate risk management. Briefly, a VAR calculation measures the sensitivity of a corporation's earnings to probable financial developments.[7] VAR calculations are made on the assumption that price and rate fluctuations in the future will be broadly similar to price and rate fluctuations in the recent past.

VAR is a conceptually simple measure of the impact of prices, rates, and operating changes on a firm's bottom line. It is a confidence interval test that, in effect, estimates the probable range of firm earnings. To illustrate VAR with a simplified, but specific, example, assume that a corporation's earnings are largely a function of the daily price at which it sells its widgets and that this price is determined in a competitive marketplace that the producer does not control. Furthermore, assume that daily widget prices are approximately normally distributed around a mean or expected price equal to the current price of the product. With price as the only variable, price fluctuations translate directly into earnings fluctuations, and the firm can calculate its daily value or earnings at risk.

As noted, VAR is a confidence interval concept. An important characteristic of the standard normal distribution is that two-thirds of all observations—prices and earnings levels in this example—fall within one standard deviation on either side of the mean, 95 percent fall within two standard deviations, and 99 percent fall within three. Because adverse earnings effects fall on one side of the mean, a two standard deviation interval on the downside includes all but the 2.5 percent or so of cases when the firm could expect worse earnings than the mean or expected earnings level minus two standard deviations. These relationships are illustrated in **Figure 6.1**. If management wanted to estimate the income level that would be exceeded about 95 percent of the time, the

---

[7]VAR is called by a variety of names, including earnings at risk (EAR), daily earnings at risk (DEAR), dollars at risk (DAR), and sterling at risk (SAR).

Figure 6-1. VAR (Daily-Earnings-at-Risk) Diagram

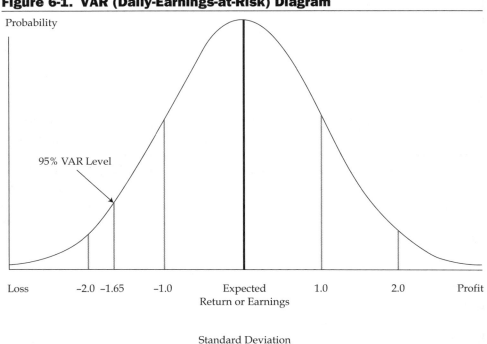

critical point would be near the 1.65 standard deviation level on the downside. Some users stress the 1.65 standard deviation level, and others stress two standard deviations. As yet, no clear consensus exists.[8]

This brief and simplified explanation of VAR—in this case, its most common variant, daily earnings at risk—can serve as the basis for a more comprehensive look at what is behind VAR. An analyst needs to know how this calculation can be useful in the analysis of the firm's risk exposures and when this calculation can give misleading results. The example we use for illustration is oversimplified because it assumes that a single underlying variable—the price of the firm's product—determines corporate financial results. In reality, selling prices, sales volumes, and the cost of various production inputs interact with financial prices and rates to determine the corporate bottom line. Some prices, costs, and rates are relatively independent of one another, and others are correlated to varying degrees. Getting all these values and relationships right is not easy, but a moment's reflection will verify

---

[8]In statistics, and in much risk management literature, standard deviation is often represented by the lower case Greek letter sigma (σ).

that the usefulness of a VAR calculation depends on the realism of the corporate earnings model.

A financial officer charged with preparing a VAR calculation can construct an earnings model based on firm-specific price and rate relationships or on a standard set of financial variables and correlations, such as the RiskMetrics database. The RiskMetrics database incorporates many of the price and rate relationships important to a financial institution or a portfolio manager, but it lacks some of the prices and relationships significant to the typical nonfinancial enterprise. Most organizations will need some data series, volatilities, and correlations unique to their operations. Nonfinancial corporations will need production or operating models and data. Firms that lack the ability to develop and maintain models and data efficiently in-house will have to rely on the services of consultants or accounting firms. Assuming satisfactory price, rate, and correlation information, calculating a daily earnings at risk number is largely a matter of supplying data to an earnings model.

A daily earnings-at-risk calculation may not reflect the most useful time interval for a particular enterprise. Nonetheless, the daily calculation is probably the most common interval for financial intermediaries. The earliest users of VAR were financial firms, which used daily mark to market before they heard of VAR. Fortunately, with some adjustment, the daily VAR calculation usually can serve as the basis for a useful analysis of risk in nonfinancial corporations as well. One of the outstanding characteristics of VAR is that an analyst familiar with standard statistical techniques and distribution relationships should be able to evaluate the assumptions behind the VAR calculation—given access to the supporting data and familiarity with the firm's operations—and extend the one-day analysis to a longer interval.

Extending a one-day earnings or VAR calculation to a longer interval is not, as some VAR discussions suggest, a simple matter of multiplying a daily VAR value by the square root of the number of days in the period chosen. A distribution may be "well behaved" over a one-day interval but very unusual over a longer time period. The best way to appreciate the limitations of VAR methodology is to look at vulnerabilities in VAR's standard assumptions in some extreme cases, and extending a one-day model to a longer period is a good place to start. A variety of techniques is used to deal with nonstandard distributions, but the bottom line is that the shape of the distribution is not usually very important, even over a longer time interval, if the volatility or standard deviation measurement is essentially correct.

Of far more consequence, in most circumstances, is the possibility that one or more volatility or correlation inputs is off the mark. For example, the stock market crash of October 1987, any number of oil price shocks, and interest rate movements in response to currency changes or central bank policy moves—all recall periods when the volatility of one or more risk inputs was substantially greater than a long-term historical analysis might suggest would be appropriate or realistic. More than one observer has noted that 15 or 20 sigma (standard deviation) events, which should not occur once in many people's lifetimes, seem to crop up every few years.

With rare exceptions, the value and correlation inputs to a VAR calculation are recent historical volatilities and correlations, often exponentially weighted to increase the impact of volatility for the most recent few days or few weeks. With exponential weighting, a change in the market volatilities will be reflected in the VAR calculation very quickly. On the other hand, a volatility shock will not be anticipated in a VAR calculation unless the volatility-estimating mechanism is designed to forecast changes in volatility and succeeds in doing so. The interaction of volatility and correlation and their changes over time can lead to substantial fluctuations in the VAR inputs.

An investment manager computing the VAR of a portfolio in early October 1987 would probably have incorporated a long-term positive correlation between stock and bond market performance. During the crash of October 19, 1987, stock and bond price correlations became negative, and a balanced portfolio did relatively well. In contrast to that period's negative correlations between stock and bond prices, correlations between stock markets in different countries increased. The risk reduction from diversification among equity markets was less than a longer-term correlation analysis would have suggested.

Unfortunately, much of the emphasis on VAR calculations has emphasized getting a single, "comparable" number for every corporation by using prescribed assumptions. This standardized approach does not take advantage of one of the best features of VAR—the ease with which an analyst can compare the results under different assumptions and evaluate the realism of these assumptions. The VAR calculation helps break down the risk components to estimate the sensitivity of the outcome to various assumptions. One can easily see how the VAR calculation can lead to a poor estimate, particularly to an underestimate of the earnings risk that the firm faces. Beder (1995), Jorion (1996), Dowd (1999), Leander (1999), and especially *Risk Management* (1999) are good places for analysts to start educating themselves on VAR. Analysts following financial intermediaries should also be familiar with the issues discussed in Kupiec (1999).

The VAR calculation is a static test based on relatively stable assumed inputs—specifically, stable means and stable volatilities. Monte Carlo simulations and scenario analyses can loosen the ties between the variables and permit the mean values of each variable to fluctuate within and beyond a typical range. Best practice among risk managers calls for a VAR calculation daily or nearly so. Scenario analyses and Monte Carlo simulations are usually performed at less frequent intervals, and when they highlight problems, they are accorded greater weight.

The Analyst's Role

The analyst should try to learn the sensitivity of financial results to the provisions of SFAS No. 133 during the risk management interview. In other words, for the firm in question, what kind of unsystematic variability in earnings will the new reporting requirements create? In the early months after implementation, the extent to which a firm has evaluated the likely impact of SFAS No. 133 on the variability of earnings, on hedging policies, and so forth will provide the analyst with a useful insight into the scope of management planning. Industry analysts will want to compare and evaluate their firms in terms of the scope of each firm's reactions to SFAS No. 133. Of particular interest will be management's initial expectations for impacts and opportunities compared with the accuracy of those expectations after a few reporting periods have gone by. An astute management will probably anticipate SFAS No. 133 questions and develop an analyst presentation based on the work of its risk management group and/or its accounting firm. As is usually the case in the work of a financial analyst, there is not a single right answer or a single right approach. Obviously, some general principles apply, and the analyst will be called on to evaluate the critical issues for each firm.

Management is the exercise of judgment. Judgment, in turn, relies on the ability of the human mind to comprehend a set of inputs and the effect of a decision on the ultimate outcome. Managers have traditionally believed that they can get their arms around the decision-making process when they understand the environment in which they operate. Growing globalization of most business enterprises, introduction and implementation of complex quantitative tools, increasingly complicated problems of regulation, human relations, and competition make it more and more difficult for a human mind to grasp the range of issues that must be evaluated in reaching business decisions.

Experience is essential, and some quantitative tools are useful in grasping the range of issues affecting a decision. Nonetheless, it is increasingly difficult for a single human mind aided by any presently available set of tools to comprehend all the issues impinging on global risk management processes. One of the most important functions of risk management is to recognize the increasing complexity of decision-making relationships and to obtain support from various segments of the organization, when support is necessary.

In conversations with a firm's shareholder-relations staff or, preferably, with the risk management staff, a financial analyst should be able to learn what risk management functions are in place, how management expects the risk management process to work today, and how management expects it to develop over time. The natural links of risk management to traditional financial analysis should qualify a securities analyst to get to the heart of the process and provide more value added to his or her clients by using risk management inquiries than with more traditional lines of questioning.

An industry analyst interviewing a corporate risk manager should go into the meeting with a comprehensive understanding of the major financial, economic, industry, and commodity risks that the specific enterprise faces. An interview with a risk manager should confirm most parts of this knowledge. The value of the interview will depend on the analyst's ability to quantify some of the risk exposures he or she expects to find and to learn how the firm has dealt or plans to deal with its exposures. The analyst's principal objective is to learn what the net exposures are or will be after management implements its risk adjustment plans. Many firms will discover as part of their risk analysis process that they face a few risks that neither they nor the financial community has fully appreciated. The analyst will want to learn about these and about the steps being taken to cope with them. After a comprehensive interview with the risk management staff at each firm followed, the analyst should know which firms will do well and which will have problems in any specific macroeconomic or geopolitical environment.

Risk managers will need to develop internal rules and procedures designed to contain or counter unacceptable risk exposures. The analyst needs to understand what the net exposures will be, based on the assumption that these procedures are followed. The analyst also needs to explore, at least briefly, what might happen if the rules are not followed. Such detection will be difficult for an outside analyst and even for a firm's management staff, and there may be incentives and/or opportunities for specific individuals to work around or evade the risk management process. Some procedures may not provide adequate scope for ensuring compliance. The analyst's best chance to detect serious problems that might stem from a risk management process that is theoretically sound but ignored or frustrated by part of the organization is to compare the comments of all contacts within a firm and compare policies and procedures between companies within an industry. Detecting problems before they occur is usually difficult, but anticipating problems and warning investors is how analysts become heroes.

References

Beder, Tanya Styblo. 1995. "VAR: Seductive but Dangerous." *Financial Analysts Journal,* vol. 51, no. 5 (September/October):12–24.

Bodie, Zvi, and Robert C. Merton. 2000. *Finance.* Upper Saddle River, NJ: Prentice Hall.

Bodnar, Gordon M., Gregory S. Hayt, and Richard C. Marston. 1996. "1995 Wharton Survey of Derivatives Usage by U.S. Non-Financial Firms." *Financial Management*, vol. 25, no. 4 (Winter):113–133.

———. 1998. "1998 Wharton Survey of Financial Risk Management by U.S. Non-Financial Firms." *Financial Management*, vol. 27, no. 4 (Winter):70–91.

Bodnar, Gordon M., Gregory S. Hayt, Richard C. Marston, and Charles W. Smithson. 1995. "Wharton Survey of Derivatives Usage by U.S. Non-Financial Firms." *Financial Management*, vol. 24, no. 2 (Summer):104–114.

Brown, Keith C., and Donald J. Smith. 1990. "Forward Swaps, Swap Options, and the Management of Callable Debt." *Journal of Applied Corporate Finance*, vol. 2, no. 4 (Winter):59–71.

Chew, Lillian. 1996. *Managing Derivative Risks: The Use and Abuse of Leverage.* New York: John Wiley & Sons.

Crabbe, Leland E., and Joseph D. Argilagos. 1994. "Anatomy of the Structured Note Market." *Journal of Applied Corporate Finance*, vol. 7, no. 3 (Fall):85–98.

Cummins, J. David, Richard D. Phillips, and Stephen D. Smith. 1998. "The Rise of Risk Management." *Federal Reserve Bank of Atlanta Economic Review* (First Quarter):30–40.

Dolde, Walter. 1993. "The Trajectory of Corporate Financial Risk Management." *Journal of Applied Corporate Finance*, vol. 6, no. 3 (Fall):33–41.

Dowd, Kevin. 1999. "Financial Risk Management." *Financial Analysts Journal,* vol. 55, no. 4 (July/August):65–71.

Financial Accounting Standards Board. 1998a. *Continuing Professional Education: A Review of Statement 133, Accounting for Derivative Instruments and Hedging Activities*. Norwalk, CT: Financial Accounting Standards Board of the Financial Accounting Foundation.

———. 1998b. *Special Report*. Stamford, CT: Financial Accounting Standards Board of the Financial Accounting Foundation.

Froot, Kenneth A., David S. Scharfstein, and Jeremy C. Stein. 1993. "Risk Management: Coordinating Corporate Investment and Financing Policies." *Journal of Finance*, vol. 48, no. 5 (December):1629–58.

———. 1994. "A New Approach to Risk Management." *Harvard Business Review* (November/December):91–102.

Gastineau, Gary L., and Mark P. Kritzman. 1999. *Dictionary of Financial Risk Management*. New Hope, PA: Frank J. Fabozzi Associates.

Gay, Gerald D., and Jouahn Nam. 1998. "The Underinvestment Problem and Corporate Derivatives Use." *Financial Management*, vol. 27, no. 4 (Winter):53–69.

Hendricks, Darryll. 1996. "Evaluation of Value-at-Risk Models Using Historical Data." *Federal Reserve Bank of New York Economic Policy Review*, vol. 2, no. 1 (April):39–69.

Hendricks, Darryll, and Beverly Hirtle. 1997. "Bank Capital Requirements for Market Risk: The Internal Models Approach." *Federal Reserve Bank of New York Economic Policy Review*, vol. 3, no. 4 (December):1–12.

Hunter, Robert. 1999. "The Accounting Standard from Outer Space." *Derivatives Strategy*, vol. 4, no. 9 (September):16–23.

Ittoop, Vinita, and Ira G. Kawaller. 1999. "Implementing FAS 133: From Theory to Practice." *TMA Journal*, vol. 19, no. 5 (September/October).

Jorion, Philippe. 1995. *Big Bets Gone Bad: Derivatives and Bankruptcy in Orange County*. San Diego, CA: Academic Press.

———. 1996. "Risk^2: Measuring the Risk in Value at Risk." *Financial Analysts Journal*, vol. 52, no. 6 (November/December):47–56.

———. 1997. *Value at Risk*. Chicago, IL: Irwin Professional Publishing.

Kawaller, Ira G., and Paul Koch. 2000. "Meeting the 'Highly Effective Expectation' Criterion for Hedge Accounting." *Journal of Derivatives*, vol. 7, no. 4 (Summer):79–87.

Kupiec, Paul H. 1999. "Risk Capital and VAR." *Journal of Derivatives,* vol. 7, no. 2 (Winter):41–52.

Leander, Tom. 1999. "A Bridge Too VAR." *Treasury & Risk Management* (November/December):50–54.

Louis, Jack. 2000. "Phantom Volatility and FAS 133." *Risk* (January):70–72.

Modigliani, Franco, and Merton H. Miller. 1958. "The Cost of Capital, Corporate Finance, and the Theory of Investment." *American Economic Review* (June):261–297.

Nance, Deana R., Clifford W. Smith, Jr., and Charles W. Smithson. 1993. "On the Determinants of Corporate Hedging." *Journal of Finance*, vol. 48, no. 1:267–284.

Overdahl, James, and Barry Schachter. 1995. "Derivatives Regulation and Financial Management: Lessons from Gibson Greetings." *Financial Management*, vol. 24, no. 1 (Spring):68–78.

PricewaterhouseCoopers LLP. 1998. *A Guide to Accounting for Derivative Instruments and Hedging Activities: Understanding & Implementing Statement of Financial Accounting Standards No. 133.*

Reiner, Eric L. 2000. "Dithering over Disclosure." *Treasury & Risk Management* (March):43–44.

Risk Management: Principles and Practices. 1999. Charlottesville, VA: AIMR.

Smith, Clifford W., and René M. Stulz. 1985. "The Determinants of Firms' Hedging Policies." *Journal of Financial and Quantitative Analysis*, vol. 20, no. 4 (December):391–405.

Smith, Donald J. 1997. "Aggressive Corporate Finance: A Close Look at the Procter & Gamble–Bankers Trust Leveraged Swap." *Journal of Derivatives*, vol. 4, no. 4 (Summer):67–79.

Stulz, René M. 1996. "Rethinking Risk Management." *Journal of Applied Corporate Finance*, vol. 9, no. 3 (Fall):8–24.

Tufano, Peter. 1996. "Who Manages Risk? An Empirical Examination of Risk Management Practices in the Gold Mining Industry." *Journal of Finance*, vol. 51, no. 4 (September):1097–1137.

———. 1998. "Agency Costs of Corporate Risk Management." *Financial Management*, vol. 27, no. 1 (Spring):67–77.

Selected AIMR Publications

AIMR Performance Presentation Standards Handbook, 2nd edition, 1997

Alternative Investing, 1998

Asian Equity Investing, 1998

Asset Allocation in a Changing World, 1998

Credit Analysis Around the World, 1998

Currency Risk in Investment Portfolios, 1999

Derivatives in Portfolio Management, 1998

Ethical Issues for Today's Firm, 2000

Equity Research and Valuation Techniques, 1998

Frontiers in Credit-Risk Analysis, 1999

The Future of Investment Management, 1998

Global Bond Management II: The Search for Alpha, 2000

Investment Counseling for Private Clients, 1999

Investment Counseling for Private Clients II, 2000

Practical Issues in Equity Analysis, 2000

Risk Management: Principles and Practices, 1999

Standards of Practice Handbook, 8th edition, 1999

The Technology Industry: Impact of the Internet, 2000

A full catalog of publications is available on AIMR's World Wide Web site at **www.aimr.org**; or you may write to AIMR, P.O. Box 3668, Charlottesville, VA 22903 U.S.A.; call 1-804-951-5499; fax 1-804-951-5262; or e-mail **info@aimr.org** to receive a free copy. All prices are subject to change.